D0128352

Extra Cheesy
Zits

Also by Jerry Scott and Jim Borgman

Zits: Sketchbook 1

Growth Spurt: Zits Sketchbook 2

Don't Roll Your Eyes at Me, Young Man!: Zits Sketchbook 3

Are We an "Us"?: Zits Sketchbook 4

Zits Unzipped: Zits Sketchbook 5

Busted!: Zits Sketchbook 6

Road Trip: Zits Sketchbook 7

Teenage Tales: Zits Sketchbook No. 8

Thrashed: Zits Sketchbook No. 9

Pimp My Lunch: Zits Sketchbook No. 10

Are We Out of the Driveway Yet?: Zits Sketchbook No. 11

Rude, Crude, and Tattooed: Zits Sketchbook No. 12

Jeremy and Mom

Pierced

Lust and Other Uses for Spare Hormones

Jeremy & Dad

You're Making That Face Again

Drive!

Triple Shot, Double Pump, No Whip Zits

Zits en Concert

Peace, Love, and Wi-Fi

Zits Apocalypse

Treasuries

Humongous Zits

Big Honkin' Zits

Zits: Supersized

Random Zits

Crack of Noon

Alternative Zits

My Bad

Sunday Brunch

Gift Book

A Zits Guide to Living with Your Teenager

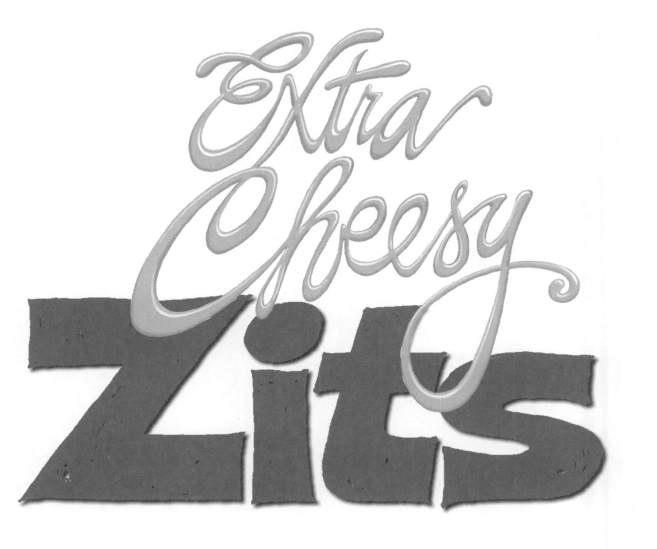

Extra Cheesy Zits

A ZITS® Treasury by Jerry Scott and Jim Borgman

Andrews McMeel Publishing®
a division of Andrews McMeel Universal

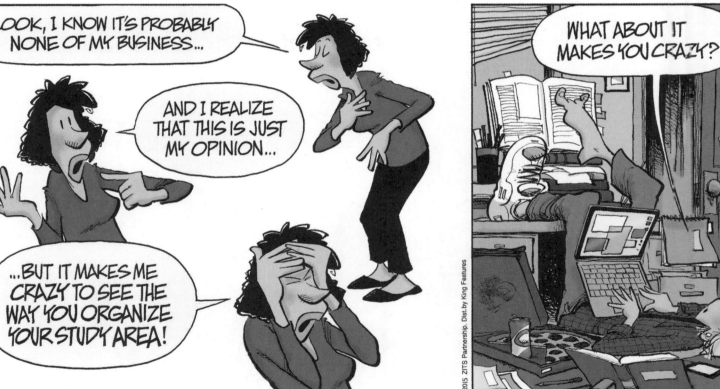

Jim: Jeremy has the messiest room and the most flexible toes in comic strip history, pending confirmation by the *Guinness Book of World Records.*

Jerry: A moment, please, to remember all the cartoonists whose blood has been spilled for our right to say "pee" on the comics page.

Jim: This poor nameless teacher shows up a lot in *Zits*. He exhibits just the right combination of cynicism and weary resignation to teach high school.

Jerry: Generally good advice for anybody when company's coming.

Jim: Why would anybody sleep with one foot in the air? Beats me.

©2015 ZITS Partnership. Dist. by King Features

THUMP! THUMP!
THUMP!
SCOTT and BORGMAN 1/12

©2015 ZITS Partnership. Dist. by King Features

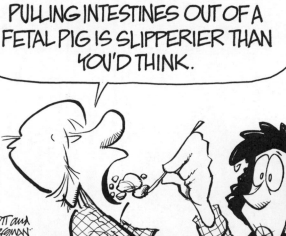

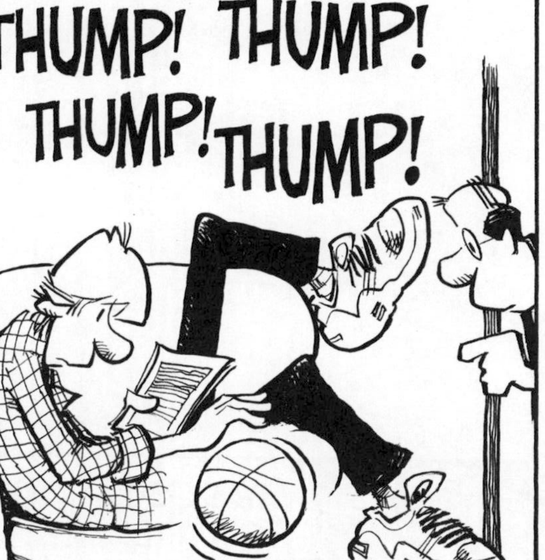
THUMP! THUMP!
THUMP! THUMP!

HE EVEN **READS** LOUDLY!
CAN'T HEAR YOU! JEREMY'S READING!

OKAY... WELL... UM...

©2015 ZITS Partnership. Dist. by King Features

PULLING INTESTINES OUT OF A FETAL PIG IS SLIPPERIER THAN YOU'D THINK.
SCOTT and BORGMAN 1/13

WELL, WE **DID** TELL HIM TO MAKE CONVERSATION AT THE TABLE...

Jim: Nice pucker, Mom.

Jerry: Parents wrote us asking what this meant. Ask yourself: When's the last time you heard Beyoncé singing from inside a backpack?

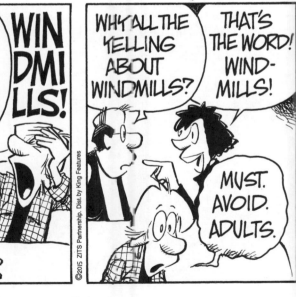

Jim: The entire secret behind *Zits* is that Jerry and I just try to crack each other up. Mission accomplished, partner.

Jim: There's a guy who sweeps up roadkill on our county highways. I'll bet you anything he has to enter them into a database.

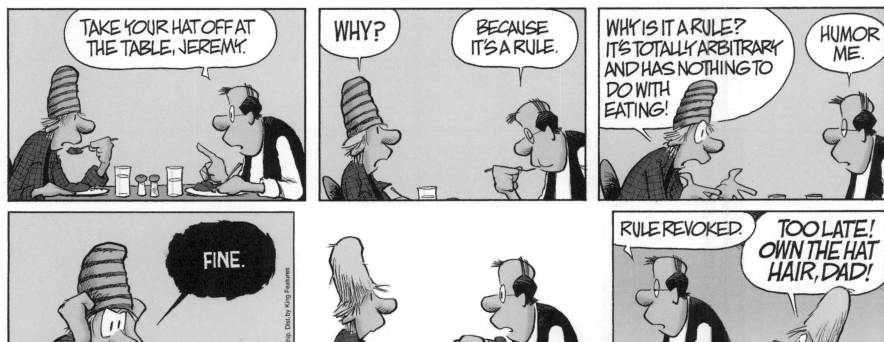

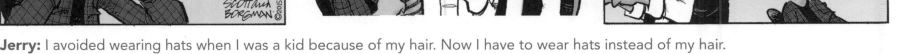

Jerry: I avoided wearing hats when I was a kid because of my hair. Now I have to wear hats instead of my hair.

©2015 ZITS Partnership. Dist. by King Features

Jim: Now I feel stuffed.

©2015 ZITS Partnership. Dist. by King Features

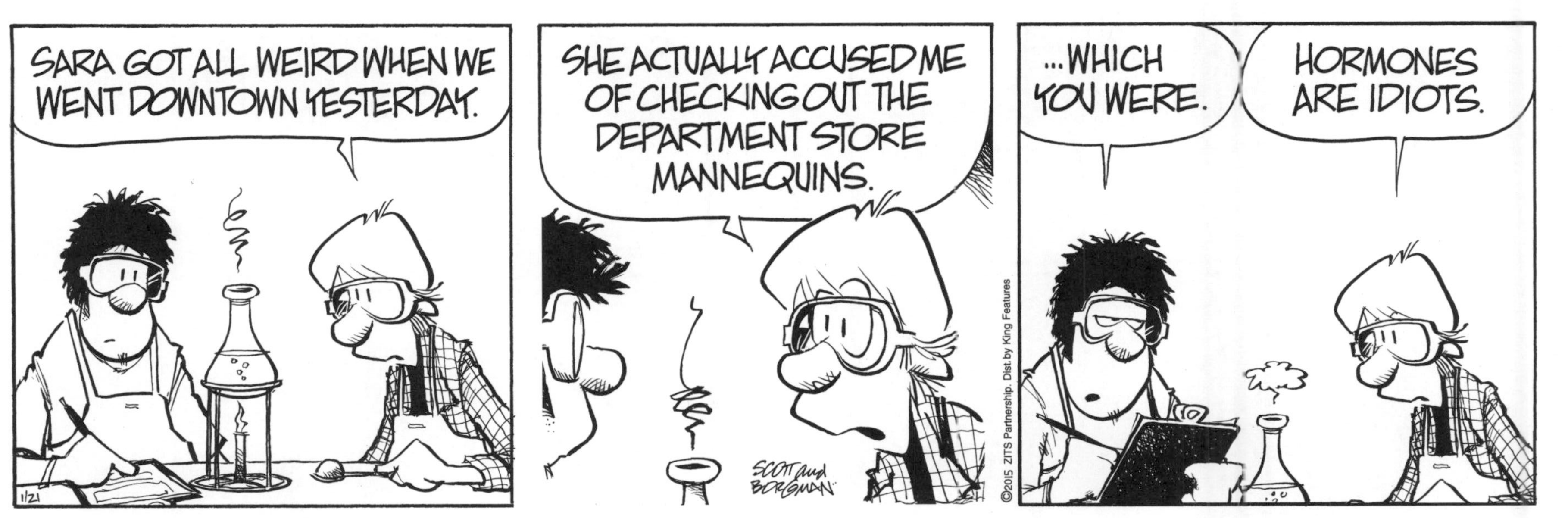

Jim: Just the sort of topic guys bond over in chem lab.

Jim: We need to do more of these. Maybe a couple of pages from now.

MY DAD'S GASTRO-INTESTINAL SYSTEM IS A FORCE OF NATURE.
GURGLE
BLURP!
SPREEENK!

HIS GUT EMITS SOUNDS AND GASSES FOUND NOWHERE ELSE IN NATURE.
SQUEEN!
GRUNK!
BLONG!
BRRRP!
SKNNXXXX
TWEEEEEE!

Jim: A fart joke on a Sunday—are we rebels or what?

MY MOM SAYS IT'S BEEN LIKE THIS SINCE HE TURNED FORTY.
PFFFF
FOO!
WHPP
WHPP
WHPP
SCOTT and BORGMAN
©2015 ZITS Partnership. Dist. by King Features
AT LEAST I THINK SHE SAID "FORTY."
IS THAT WITH AN "O" OR AN "A"?
1/25

Jerry: How DID we get away with that?

©2015 ZITS Partnership. Dist. by King Features

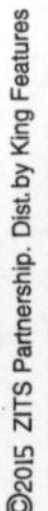
©2015 ZITS Partnership. Dist. by King Features

Jim: Nothing can kill an appetite like a dad playing Led Zeppelin on air guitar. Except maybe a mom dancing to Rod Stewart.

©2015 ZITS Partnership. Dist. by King Features

Jerry: "The new phonebook's here! The new phonebook's here!" I couldn't get that Steve Martin line from *The Jerk* out of my head when I was working on this strip.

©2015 ZITS Partnership. Dist. by King Features

Jim: ". . . and don't forget to floss."

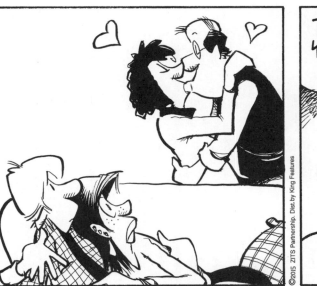

Jim: A little space, please. There's a reason God created finished basements.

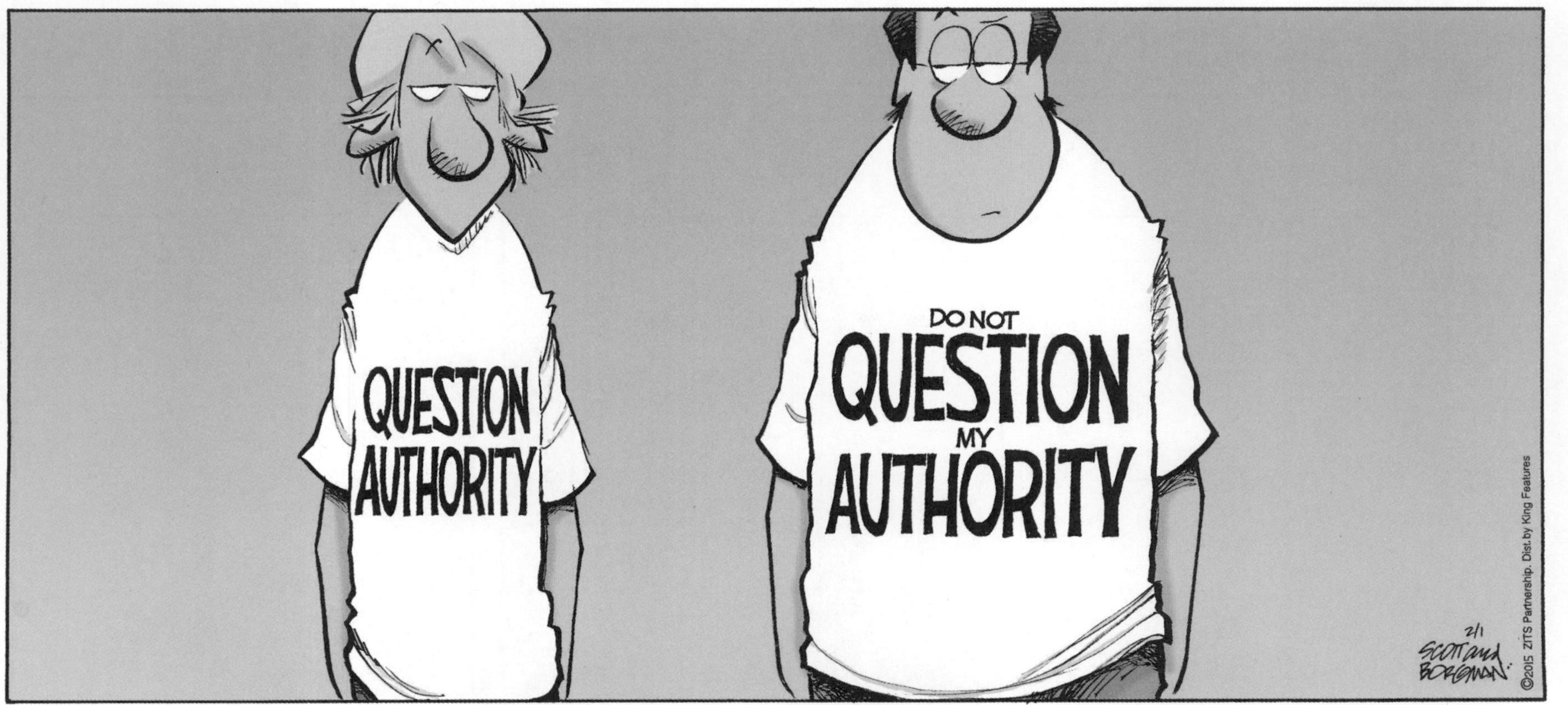

Jerry: Full disclosure: I did a form of this joke in *Baby Blues* about twenty years ago, way before I had teenagers. Later it seemed too good not to reprise in *Zits*.

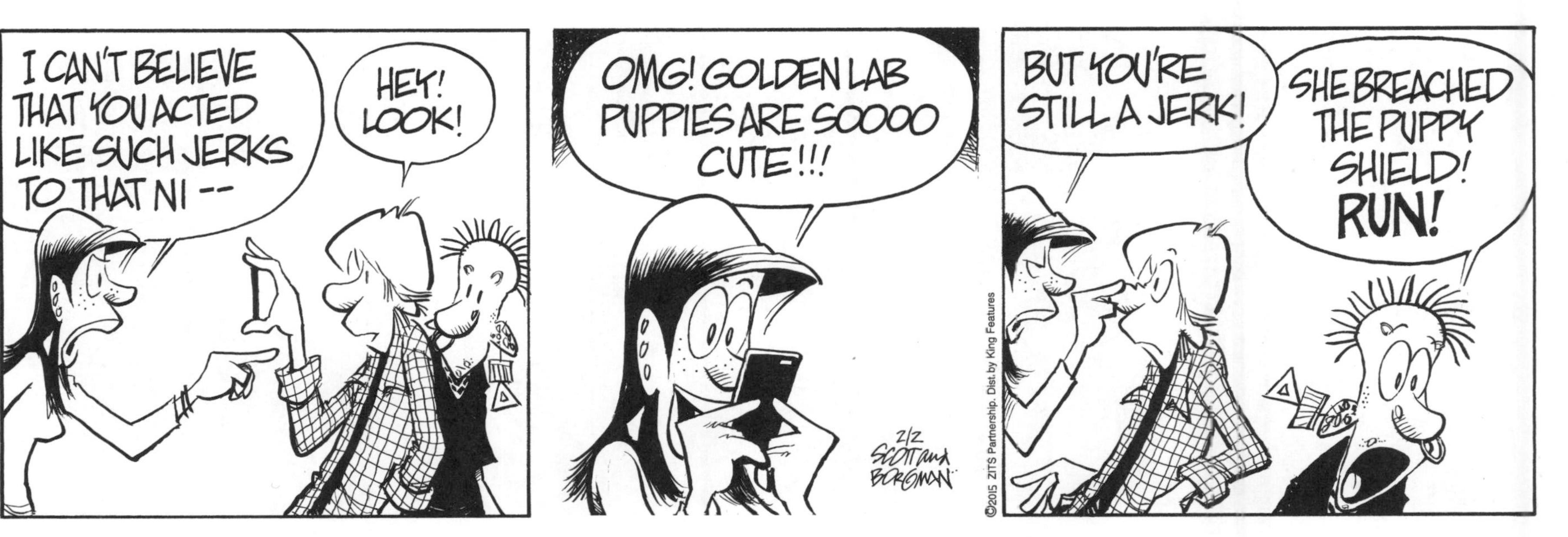

Jim: Ah, car bingo. Those were the days.

©2015 ZITS Partnership. Dist. by King Features

©2015 ZITS Partnership. Dist. by King Features

Jerry: *Zits* is published in something like forty-five languages. Therefore, we never use puns. Except that day.

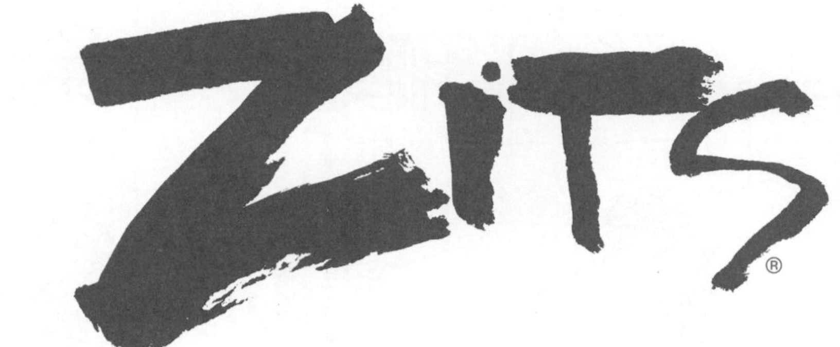

by JERRY SCOTT and
JIM BORGMAN

HEY MOM! CHECK IT OUT!
(GASP!)

THEY'RE EARRINGS I BOUGHT SARA FOR VALENTINE'S DAY.
OH,
MY.

THEY'RE REALLY...
...SOMETHING.

SHE'S GOING TO FREAK OUT.
POSSIBLY!
2/8
SCOTT and BORGMAN

DON'T BE SURPRISED IF SHE DECIDES TO SAVE THEM FOR A SPECIAL OCCASION.

©2015 ZITS Partnership. Dist. by King Features

LIKE CARNIVAL IN RIO.
YEAH! LIKE PROM!

Jerry: I passed on my bad jewelry-picking skills to Jeremy.

Jim: Note to teenagers: Not a good reason.

Jim: Of all the made-up gift-giving holidays, Valentine's Day ranks right up there with National Kazoo Day (January 28).

Jerry: Cartoonists get asked to draw all the cards in the family. I bet it's even worse for poets.

I NEED A CARD FOR MY GIRLFRIEND.
OKAY.
IT SHOULD SAY:
"I HOPE THIS CARD IS LESS DISAPPOINTING THAN THE ONE I GOT YOU LAST YEAR."
CHECK IN THE "FROM CLUELESS GUY" SECTION.
I DID. YOU'RE SOLD OUT.
©2015 ZITS Partnership. Dist. by King Features
2/13
SCOTT and BORGMAN

FIVE BUCKS FOR A STUPID VALENTINE'S CARD?
SERIOUSLY??
Valentine
KISS! KISS! KISS! KISS! KISS!
I LOVE, LOVE, LOVE, LOVE, LOVE, LOVE, LOVE IT!
SCOTT and BORGMAN 2/14
I'LL TAKE AT LEAST THREE.
Valentine
©2015 ZITS Partnership. Dist. by King Features

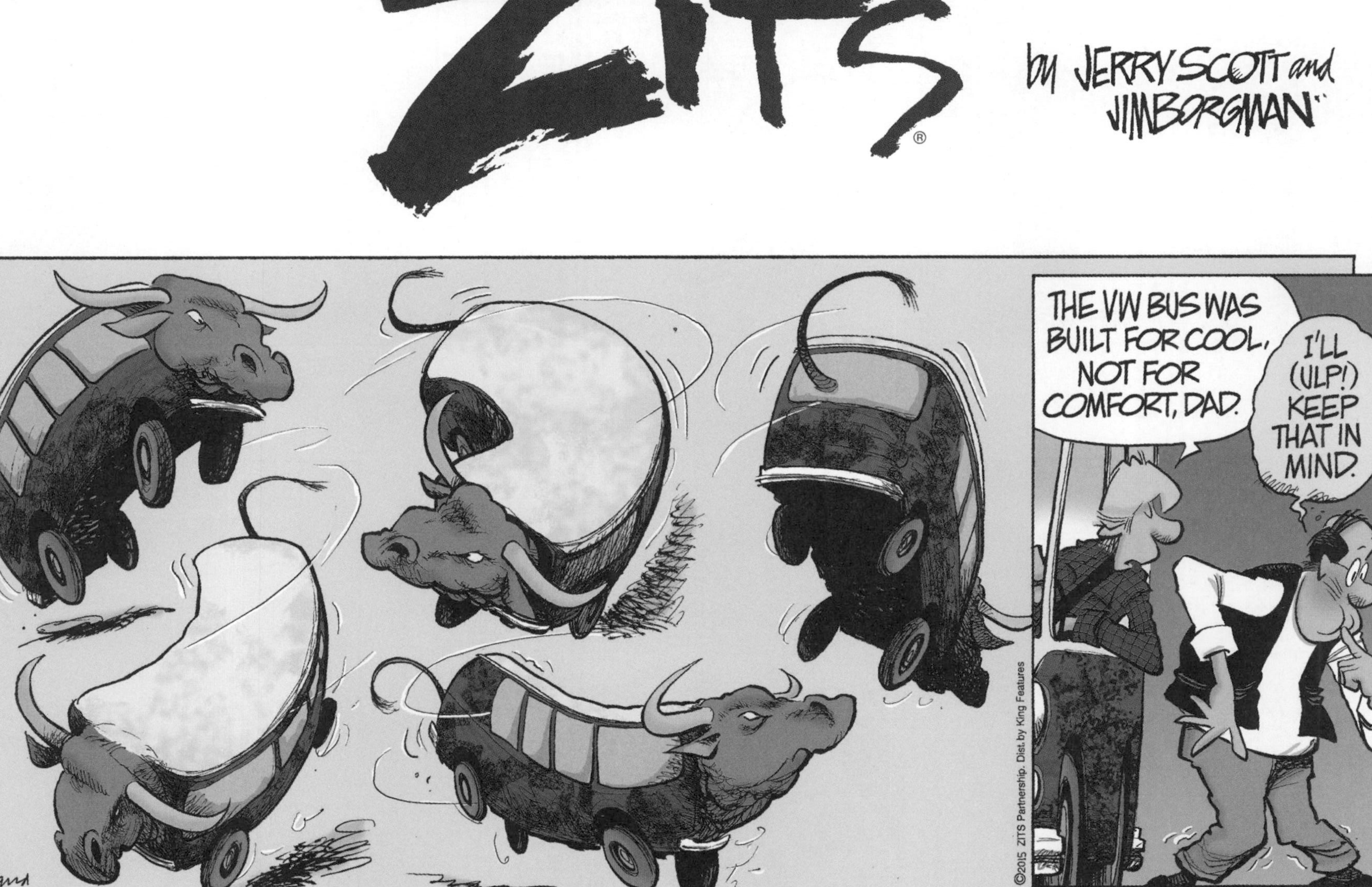

Jim: In his spare time my partner Jerry paints cows. They keep showing up in his ideas for *Zits*. Trust me, it's an improvement over his aardvark period.

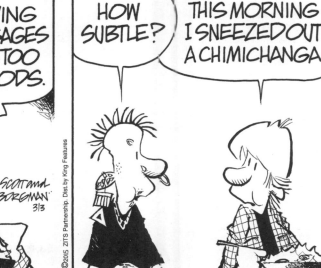

Jim: After much deliberation, we determined that "chimichanga" was funnier than "jumbo pretzel dog." This is what makes us professional humorists. Listen and learn, kids.

JEREMY, I'M WASHING A LOAD OF JEANS!
IF YOU WANT TO THROW SOMETHING IN, SEND IT DOWN!
OKAY! JUST ONE MORE BUNGEE!
3/4 SCOTT and BORGMAN
©2015 ZITS Partnership. Dist. by King Features
BUNGEE? WHY WOULD...?
HEADS UP!

Jerry: One time our washing machine flooded the house. Thinking back, it must have been revenge for me overloading it like this.

I'M REALLY PILING UP THE COMMUNITY SERVICE HOURS THIS MONTH!
GOOD FOR YOU!
©2015 ZITS Partnership. Dist. by King Features
3/5 SCOTT and BORGMAN
TODAY I RELEASED FOUR SQUIRRELS BACK INTO THE WILD.
WOULD THEY HAPPEN TO BE THE ONES WE FOUND LIVING IN YOUR CLOSET?
THE DETAILS AREN'T REALLY IMPORTANT, ARE THEY?

PIZZA'S HERE!
YES!
FINALLY!
SCOTT and BORGMAN 3/6
BUT FIRST LET'S ALL ENJOY A NICE, HEALTHY SALAD.
©2015 ZITS Partnership. Dist. by King Features
IT'S LIKE STANDING AT THE GATES OF HEAVEN AND FINDING OUT THAT YOU'RE IN BOARDING GROUP 6.

THAT'S IT, DAD!
FLAUNT IT!
YOU'RE ALL, "LOOK WHAT MY FOLLICLES CAN DO!"
©2015 ZITS Partnership. Dist. by King Features

WHO CARES?
JEREMY ENVIES MY SCRUFF.
HE DOESN'T HAVE TO KISS YOU.
3/7 SCOTT and BORGMAN

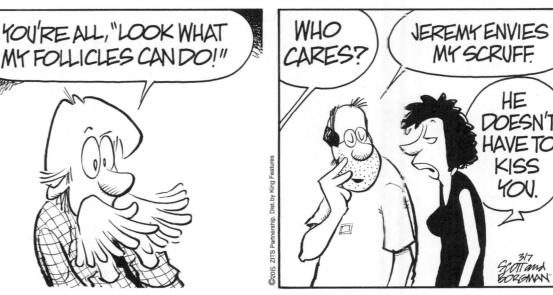

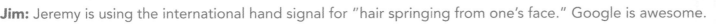

Jim: Jeremy is using the international hand signal for "hair springing from one's face." Google is awesome.

ZITS®
by JERRY SCOTT and JIM BORGMAN

PIZZA
SCOTT and BORGMAN
NUTS! I THOUGHT IT WOULD BE OVER BY NOW.
I THINK WE NEED A DRUM SOLO INTERVENTION.
2/22

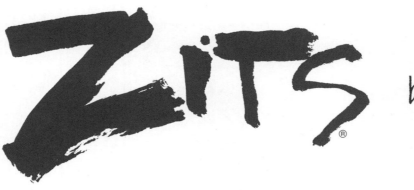

Jim: What'd I say about flexible feet?

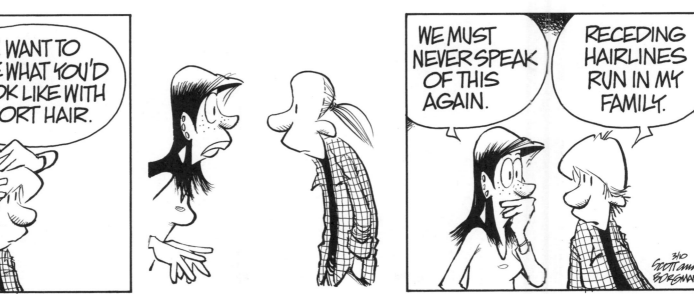

Jerry: And mine.

THE BATHROOMS AREN'T TOO BAD TODAY.

©2015 ZITS Partnership. Dist.by King Features

Jim: Reading Dante turned out to be worthwhile after all.

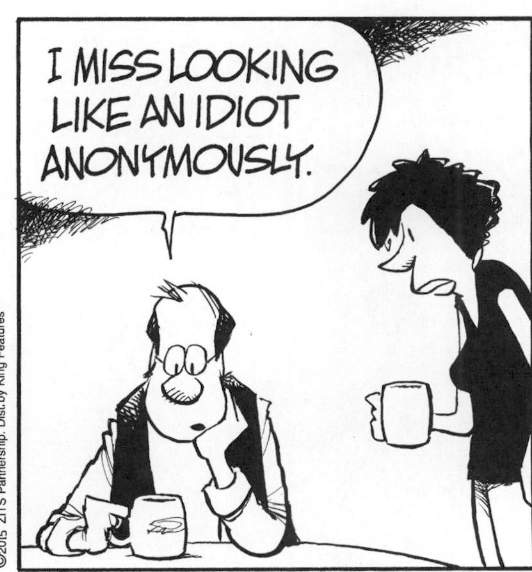
ATTIC
ATTIC
ATTIC
CLICK!

I MISS LOOKING LIKE AN IDIOT ANONYMOUSLY.

©2015 ZITS Partnership. Dist.by King Features

Jerry: #dadfail #cartoonunderwear #instagramlegend

Jim: Siri, why is my son always staring at his phone?

©2015 ZITS Partnership. Dist. by King Features

Jerry: Let's see, the outside fork is for shoveling mashed potatoes, right?

ALL IT WOULD TAKE IS A LITTLE CONCRETE AND A SLIDING WINDOW.
NO.
DAD AND I COULD DO IT IN A WEEKEND, AND I'D NEVER BE LATE FOR SCHOOL AGAIN!
SCOTT and BORGMAN 3/16

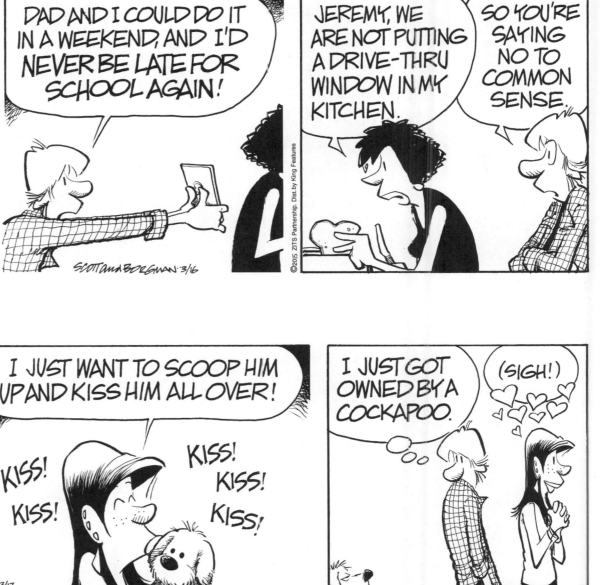

JEREMY, WE ARE NOT PUTTING A DRIVE-THRU WINDOW IN MY KITCHEN.
SO YOU'RE SAYING NO TO COMMON SENSE.
©2015 ZITS Partnership. Dist. by King Features

OHMYGAWD! LOOK AT THE PUPPY!!
©2015 ZITS Partnership. Dist. by King Features
I JUST WANT TO SCOOP HIM UP AND KISS HIM ALL OVER!
KISS!
KISS!
KISS!
KISS!
KISS!
3/17 SCOTT and BORGMAN

I JUST GOT OWNED BY A COCKAPOO.
(SIGH!)

JEREMY! DUDE! GET OVER HERE! BETHANY'S PARENTS ARE OUT OF TOWN AND SHE'S THROWING A RAGING PARTY! EVERYBODY IS HERE! HECTOR! AUTUMN! MOLLY! CHARLOTTE! D'IJON AND SARA ARE ON THEIR WAY OVER WITH THOSE SKETCHY GIRLS FROM FRENCH CLASS AND THEY'RE BRINGING SOME OF THA—
JAB! JAB! JAB!
SCOTT and BORGMAN 3/18
WRONG NUMBER.
SIT. STAY.
LOOKS LIKE ANOTHER NETFLIX NIGHT FOR YOU, SON.

©2015 ZITS Partnership. Dist. by King Features

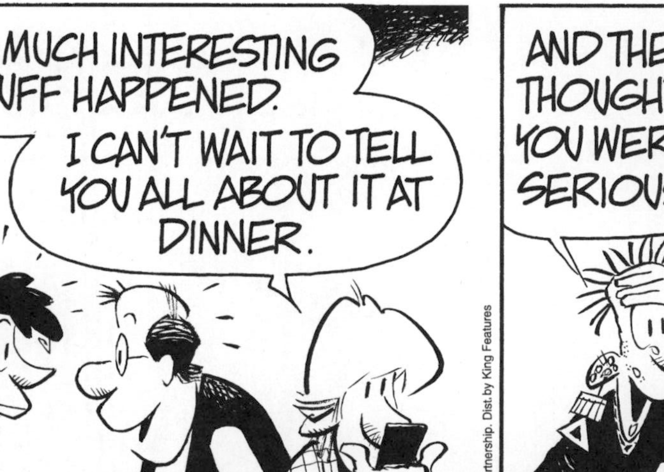

HOW WAS YOUR DAY, JEREMY?
AWESOME!
SCOTT and BORGMAN
SO MUCH INTERESTING STUFF HAPPENED.
I CAN'T WAIT TO TELL YOU ALL ABOUT IT AT DINNER.

©2015 ZITS Partnership. Dist. by King Features

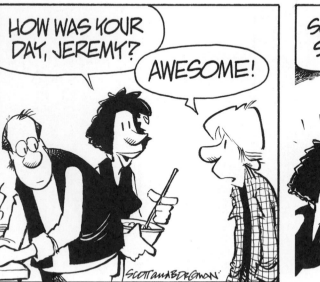

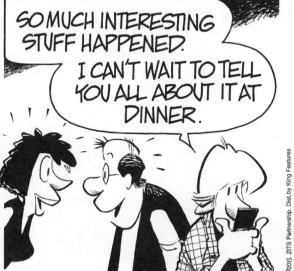

AND THEY THOUGHT YOU WERE SERIOUS?
WHAT PART OF THAT WOULD HAVE SOUNDED SINCERE TO YOU??
3/19

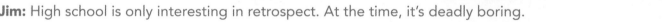

Jim: High school is only interesting in retrospect. At the time, it's deadly boring.

Jerry: I like comic strips with funny drawings and as little dialogue as possible (said the writer).

Jerry: Jim calls me on my antiquated references all the time. Here we see me getting paid for it, so there.

HOW ARE THE BOYS DOING UP THERE?
FINE.
THEY'RE LIKE SPONGES AT THIS AGE.
©2015 ZITS Partnership. Dist. by King Features

Jim: In college I minored in drawing pizza boxes, which has come in very handy.

Jerry: What kind of mysterious adhesive sticks to a teenager's gunk-coated backpack? Nice work, 3M!

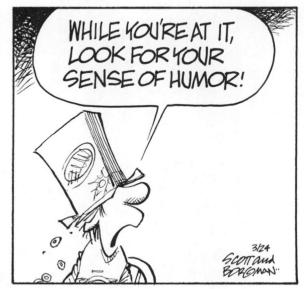

Jim: Nothing says vaudeville like the old cereal box on the head, am I right?

Jim: With the proliferation of cell phones, the phone call has become obsolete. Discuss.

SARA JUST SENT ME A SELFIE.

©2015 ZITS Partnership. Dist. by King Features

JUMP! Scrape!
JAB! SCRAMBLE!
Push!
SHOVE!
3/27
SCOTT and BORGMAN

IT'S NOT HOT.
OH, THEN NEVER MIND.

MOM, I LITERALLY HAVE A SONG STUCK IN MY HEAD.
©2015 ZITS Partnership. Dist. by King Features

JEREMY, IF THAT WERE *LITERALLY* TRUE...
3/28
SCOTT and BORGMAN

... IT WOULD LOOK LIKE THAT.
I KNOW WHAT 'LITERALLY' MEANS, MOM.

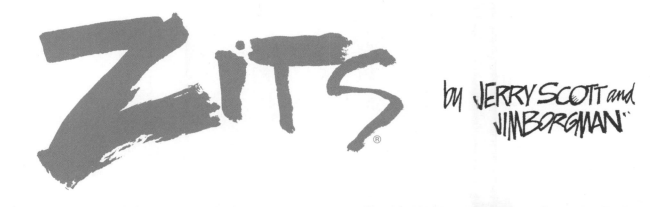

Jerry: People do stuff after 8:30 p.m.?

Jerry: A few VW bus owners wrote to remind us that running out of gas is just one of the reasons that those things often don't move.

Jim: A visually ambitious strip like this makes me mourn the shrinking of the newspaper comics page. At least on the screen you can hit the zoom button.

©2015 ZITS Partnership. Dist. by King Features

©2015 ZITS Partnership. Dist. by King Features

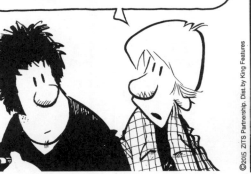

Jim: Recently I heard that lockers are becoming obsolete in some schools while backpacks are getting heavier. Does this make sense to anyone?

Jerry: miNdy0uroWnBu$1ne$$,m0M&Dad

Jim: Contortion is fun to draw.

Jim: Filters are the key to happiness. Husbands have known this for years.

Jim: Which brings us to the subject of cartoon shorthand. Nothing says "busy in the kitchen" like an apron, though no one has actually worn one since 1955.

Jim: Ha ha @jeremyduncan @saratoomey #parentsruineverything

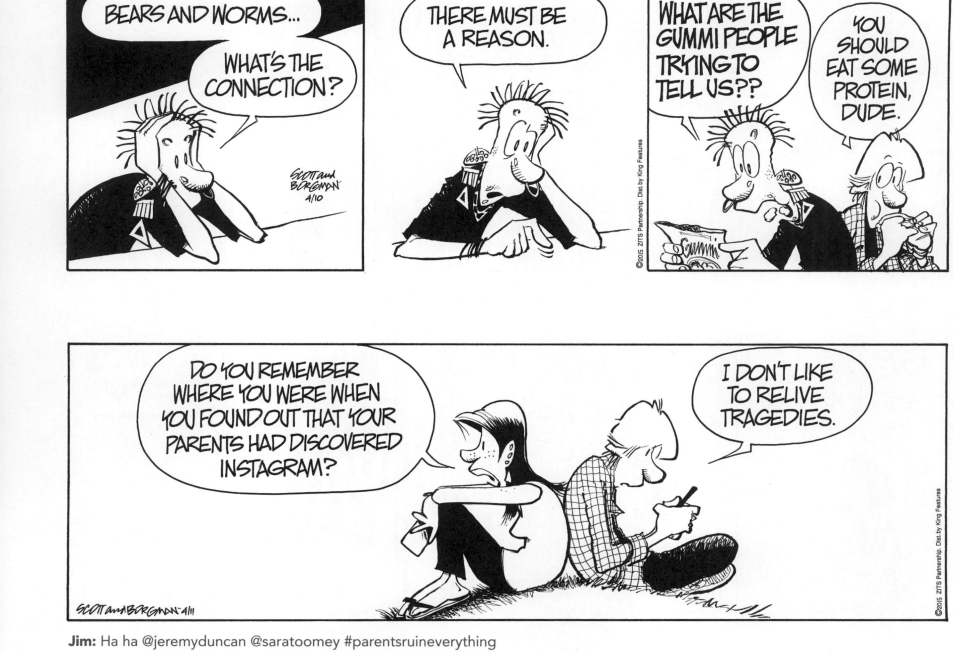

©2015 ZITS Partnership. Dist. by King Features

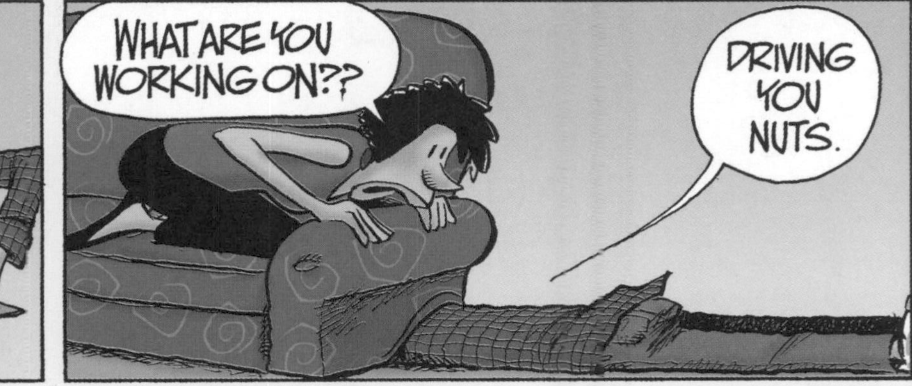

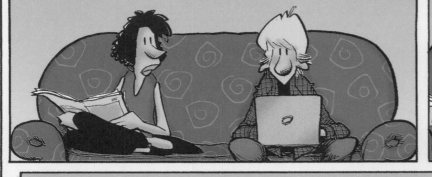

Jerry: It's funny because moms.

JEREMY, CAN Y--
SORRY, DAD, YOU'RE NOT ON THE LIST.
4/13
©2015 ZITS Partnership. Dist. by King Features
WHAT LIST?
THE LIST OF PEOPLE WHO ARE GRANTED ACCESS TO MY ROOM.
SCOTT and BORGMAN
I OWN THIS ROOM!
TELL IT TO THE LIST.
UM... CAN I GET IN THE FRIDGE?
I'M AFRAID NOT.
©2015 ZITS Partnership. Dist. by King Features
BUT I'M HUNGRY!
SORRY. YOU'RE NOT ON THE LIST.
WHAT?? THAT'S NOT FAIR!
SHALL I CALL THE BOUNCER?
OH, PLEASE DO!
SCOTT and BORGMAN 4/14

Jim: A kid I know used to win bets at school by cramming impossible amounts of food into his mouth. Okay, he was my kid.

Jim: The friend of our family who I pictured when we created Pierce has grown up to be a scuba boat captain out of Key West. Seems about right.

Jerry: Is it just me, or does everybody feel over-surveyed?

Jerry: "Let's put a polar bear and a whale in a four-by-one-inch comic strip." **Jim:** "Done."

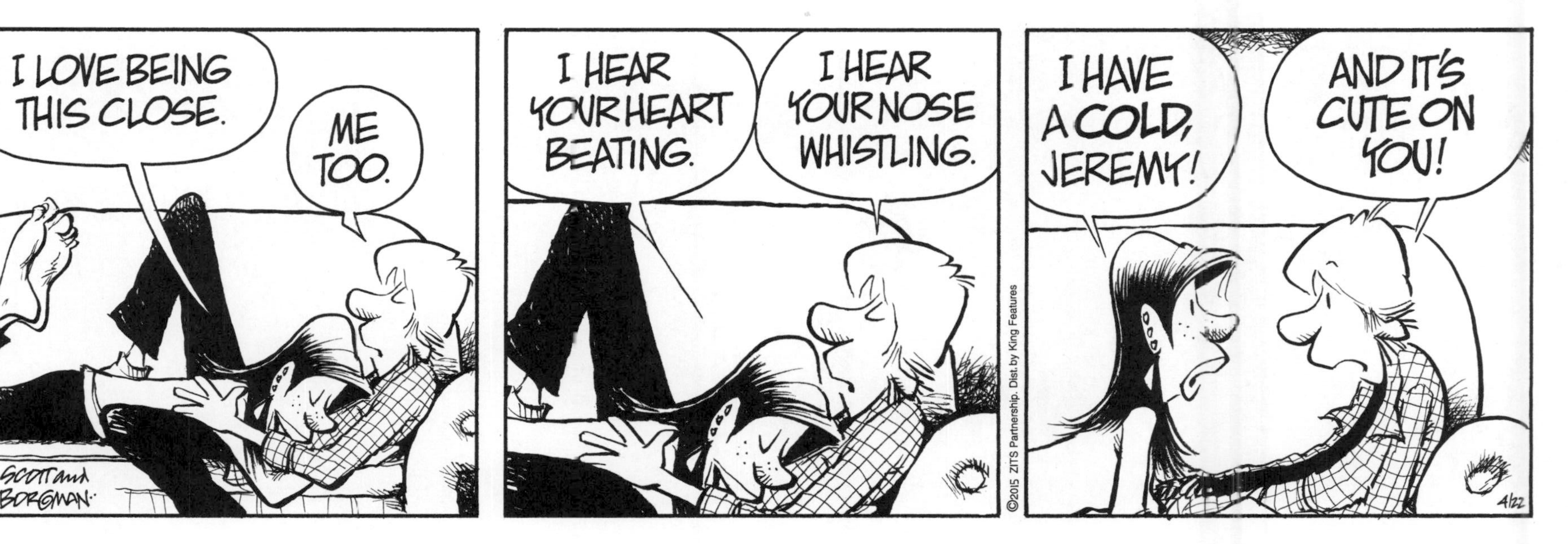
I LOVE BEING THIS CLOSE.
ME TOO.
I HEAR YOUR HEART BEATING.
I HEAR YOUR NOSE WHISTLING.
I HAVE A COLD, JEREMY!
AND IT'S CUTE ON YOU!
SCOTT and BORGMAN
4/22
©2015 ZITS Partnership. Dist. by King Features

PING! PING! PING! PING! PING!
WHO KEEPS TEXTING YOU?
I DUNNO. PROBABLY MY MOM.
PING! PING! PING! PING! PING!
4/23
SCOTT and BORGMAN
©2015 ZITS Partnership. Dist. by King Features
HER PLAN GIVES HER UNLIMITED NAGGING.
PING! PING! PING! PING! PING!

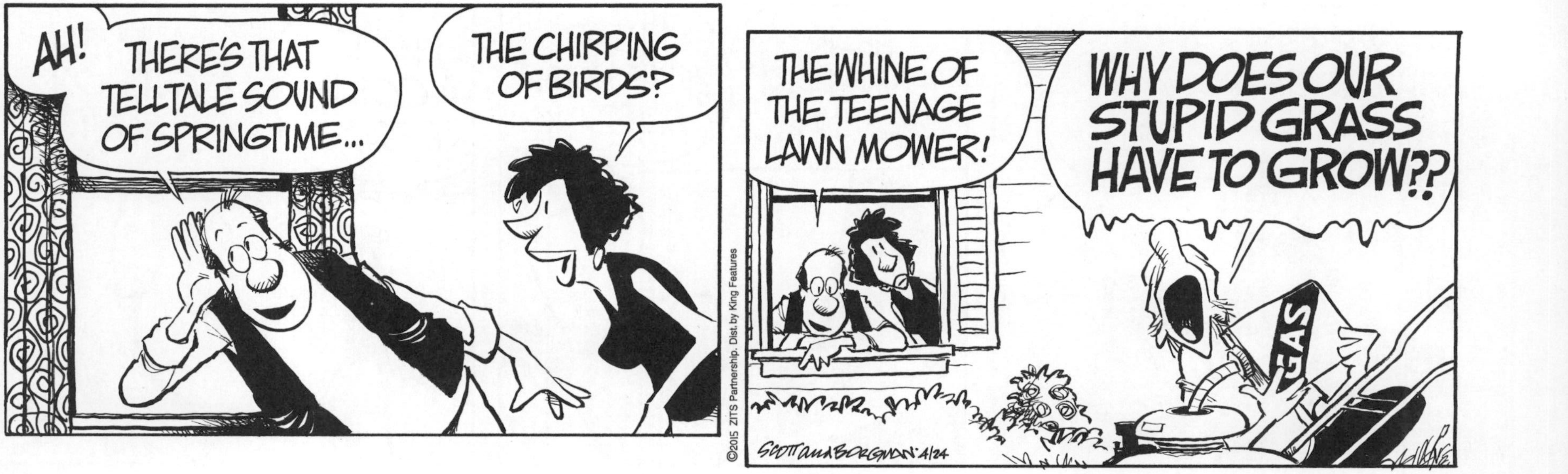

©2015 ZITS Partnership. Dist. by King Features

©2015 ZITS Partnership. Dist. by King Features

Jim: If I was going to invent something, it would be the stupid-things-I've-said-to-girls undo button.

©2015 ZITS Partnership. Dist. by King Features

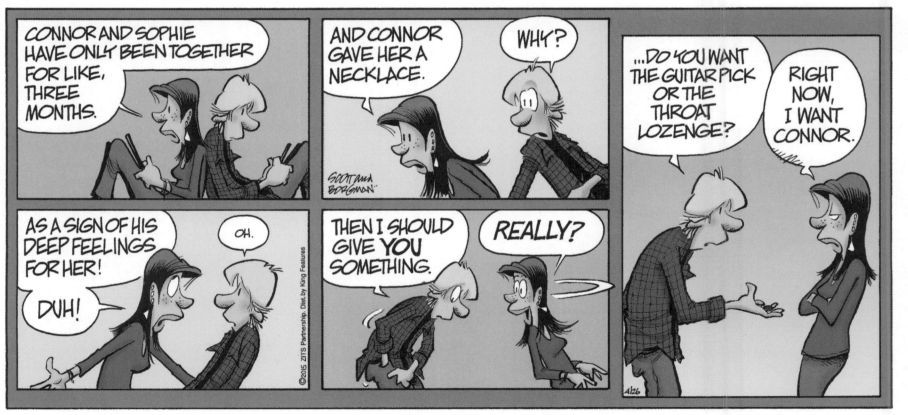

©2015 ZITS Partnership. Dist. by King Features

BLEAH!
SCOTT and BORGMAN

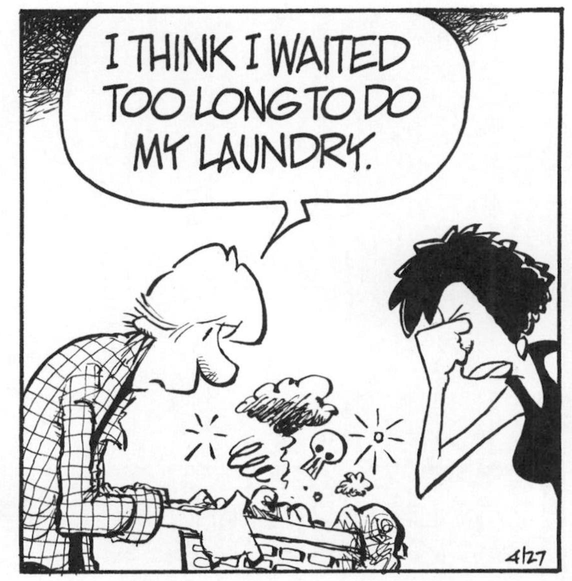
I THINK I WAITED TOO LONG TO DO MY LAUNDRY.
4/27

WIPE! WIPE! WIPE! WIPE! WIPE! WIPE!
SCOTT and BORGMAN

SPRITZ! SPRITZ!
4/28

©2015 ZITS Partnership. Dist. by King Features

WIPE! WIPE! WIPE! WIPE! WIPE! WIPE! WIPE! WIPE! WIPE! WIPE! WIPE! WIPE!

I'D CLEAN YOUR iPAD SCREEN, TOO, BUT THE PAPER TOWEL COMPANY NEEDS TO GROW A NEW FOREST FIRST.
LOOK HOW BRIGHT THE COLORS ARE!

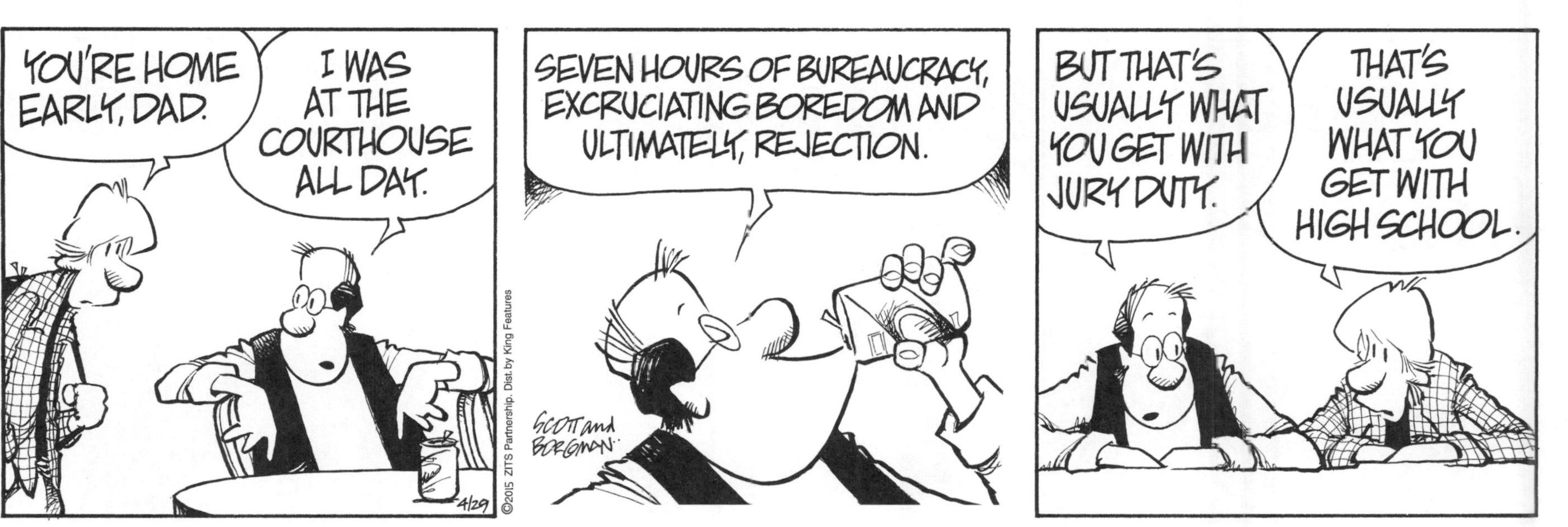

Jerry: I hope this one made it to a few teachers' lounge bulletin boards.

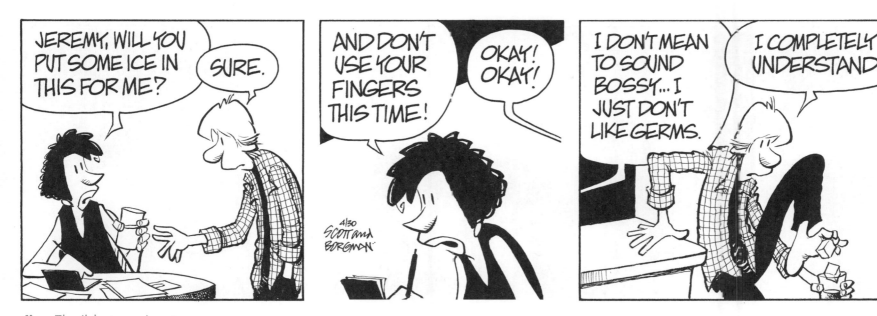

Jim: Flexible toes. I rest my case.

DUDES! CHECK OUT THIS VIDEO!

NO, WAIT--LET ME GET MY TABLET, INSTEAD.
©2015 ZITS Partnership. Dist. by King Features

SOME THINGS ARE JUST MEANT TO BE VIEWED ON THE BIG SCREEN.
SCOTT and BORGMAN
5/1

I'M HOME!
WE'RE IN THE FAMILY ROOM.
SLAM!
SCOTT and BORGMAN
©2015 ZITS Partnership. Dist. by King Features

5/2

OR, YOU COULD HAVE JUST TOSSED MY SHOES OUTSIDE.
WE'RE FRESH OUT OF TEN-FOOT POLES.

ZITS®
by JERRY SCOTT and JIM BORGMAN
WHERE ARE YOU GOING, JEREMY?
MOM TOLD ME TO GET THE MAIL.
DRESSED LIKE THAT??
YEAH.
LET ME GET IT.
OKAY.
I'M GOING TO GET THE MAIL.
DRESSED LIKE THAT??
PUSS MONKEY
HERMAN'S HERMITS
SCOTT and BORGMAN 5/3
©2015 ZITS Partnership. Dist. by King Features

MAN! SUMMER BREAK IS SO CLOSE, I CAN TASTE IT!
OH? WHAT DOES IT TASTE LIKE?

SMACK!
SMACK!
5/4 SCOTT and BORGMAN

MOSTLY FRAPPUCCINO, GUACAMOLE AND SWEAT.
I'LL PICK UP SOME BREATH MINTS.

©2015 ZITS Partnership. Dist. by King Features

IS THAT ALL YOU'VE GOT? HUH?
5/5 SCOTT and BORGMAN

I THINK I MAY STILL HAVE ONE SURVIVING TASTE BUD.
MORE SRIRACHA SAUCE, COMING UP!

©2015 ZITS Partnership. Dist. by King Features

Jerry: Angry Taste Buds. Watch for the video game.

JEREMY! YOU'RE DRIPPING WATER ALL OVER!
SORRY. I NEEDED A SNACK.
CHIPS
SALSA

WHY DIDN'T YOU DRY OFF FIRST?
I'M NOT FINISHED WITH MY SHOWER.
5/6
SCOTT and BORGMAN
©2015 ZITS Partnership. Dist. by King Features

ANY LUCK?
I'M SORRY, SWEETIE.
5/7

I CAN'T FIND ANY PHOTOS OF YOU FROM THIRD GRADE.
NONE?
SCOTT and BORGMAN

DOES THAT HURT YOUR FEELINGS?
COMING FROM A PERSON WHO TAKES PICTURES OF HER SALADS, YEAH, A LITTLE.

Jim: I've indulged two of my secret pleasures here: the Cincinnati Reds and old band T-shirts. If you've never read the old comic strip *Pogo*, look it up. Walt Kelly often slipped his friends' names onto the side of Pogo's skiff.

ZITS®
by JERRY SCOTT and JIM BORGMAN
Happy Mother's Day, Mommy!
HAPPY MOTHER
MACARONI
5/10
HAPPY MOTHERS
oh-hpy MoDay
SIGH! LIFE COMES FULL CIRCLE.
SCOTT and BORGMAN
©2015 ZITS Partnership. Dist. by King Features

THAT WAS THE BANK'S FRAUD DEPARTMENT. OUR CREDIT CARD GOT HACKED!
NOT AGAIN!

SOMEBODY TRIED TO CHARGE $6,000 IN SKI EQUIPMENT TO OUR CARD IN IDAHO!
ARE WE BROKE?

©2015 ZITS Partnership. Dist. by King Features

NO, HONEY. IT'S JUST GOING TO BE A BIG HASSLE.
WHO ARE THESE HACKERS, ANYWAY?
IDAHO... IDAHO... WHY DOES THAT SOUND FAMILIAR?
SCOTT AND BORGMAN 5/11

Jim: In my case, it was $3,000 charged to my card from a movie theater in Colorado. Who spends three grand at a movie theater?

GRRR!
CREDIT CARD FRAUD IS SUCH A HASSLE! NOW I HAVE TO RESET ALL OF OUR AUTOPAYS!

HOW DID IT HAPPEN?
WHO KNOWS? SOMEBODY ORDERS SOMETHING OFF A BOGUS WEBSITE, AND BAM! WE'RE SCREWED!
SCOTT AND BORGMAN 5/12

©2015 ZITS Partnership. Dist. by King Features

WEDOYOURHOMEWURK.com IS LEGIT, RIGHT?
HOW COULD IT NOT BE?

MOM, I THINK I SCREWED UP.
...MAYBE.
OH?
SCOTT and BORGMAN
©2015 ZITS Partnership. Dist. by King Features
REMEMBER LAST MONTH WHEN I WAS SWAMPED WITH HOMEWORK...
...AND I SAID THAT I'D LIKE TO WAVE A MAGIC WAND AND MAKE IT ALL GO AWAY?
WELL, I SORTA WAVED A MAGIC MOUSE INSTEAD.
TELL ME MORE...
5/13

YOU BOUGHT HOMEWORK ONLINE WITH MY CREDIT CARD?

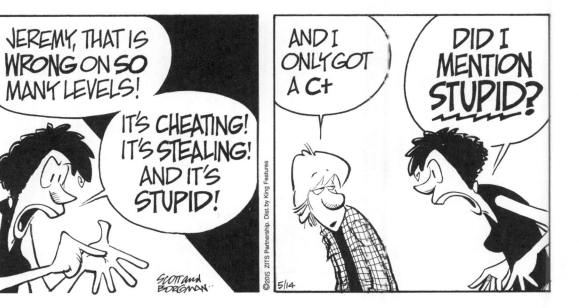

JEREMY, THAT IS WRONG ON SO MANY LEVELS!
IT'S CHEATING! IT'S STEALING! AND IT'S STUPID!
SCOTT and BORGMAN
©2015 ZITS Partnership. Dist. by King Features
AND I ONLY GOT A C+
DID I MENTION STUPID?
5/14

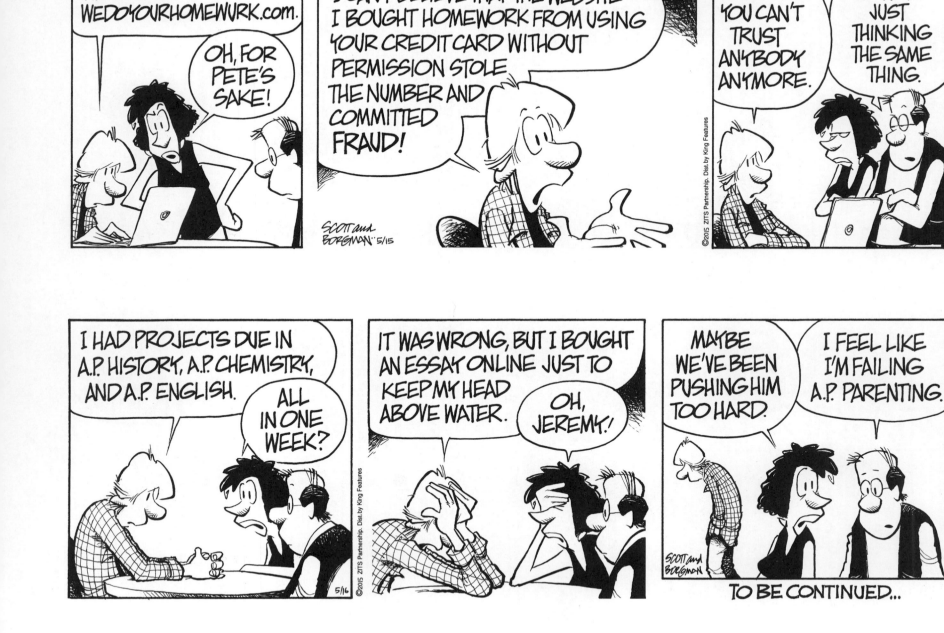

©2015 ZITS Partnership. Dist. by King Features

©2015 ZITS Partnership. Dist. by King Features

TO BE CONTINUED...

ZITS®

by JERRY SCOTT and JIM BORGMAN

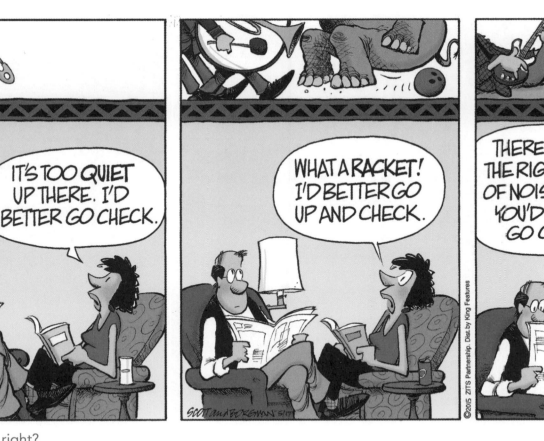

Jerry: Moms. Am I right?

©2015 ZITS Partnership. Dist. by King Features

©2015 ZITS Partnership. Dist. by King Features

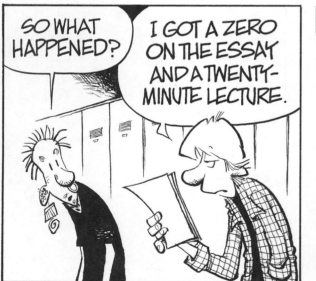

Jim: You know things have gone off the tracks when Pierce is handing out ethical advice.

©2015 ZITS Partnership. Dist. by King Features

Jerry: I wonder if it hurts to stick your arm through comic strip panels like that.

©2015 ZITS Partnership. Dist. by King Features

©2015 ZITS Partnership. Dist. by King Features

©2015 ZITS Partnership. Dist. by King Features

ZITS®

by JERRY SCOTT and JIM BORGMAN

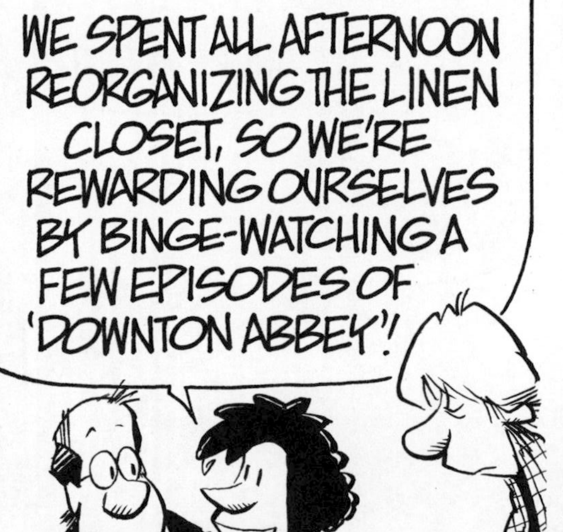

Jim: I don't know why I tell Jerry anything about my weekends.

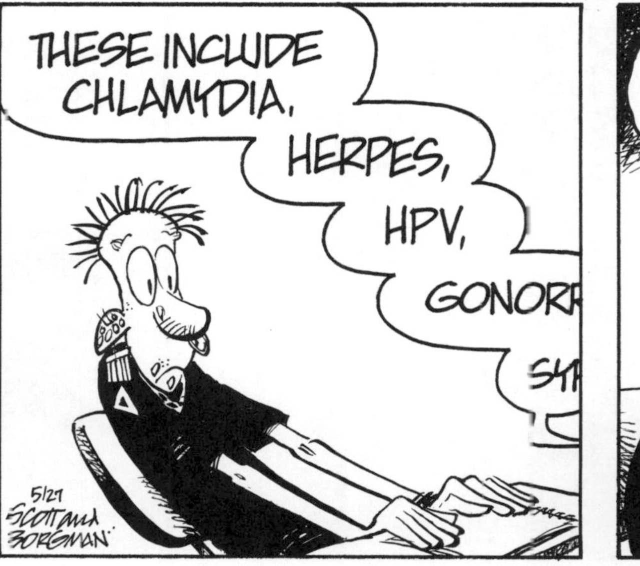

©2015 ZITS Partnership. Dist. by King Features

©2015 ZITS Partnership. Dist. by King Features

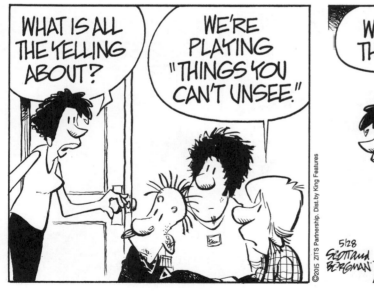

Jerry: If there are fifty Inuit words for "snow," there are ten thousand prom words for "dress."

Jim: I think we captured the post-prom look, if I do say so myself.

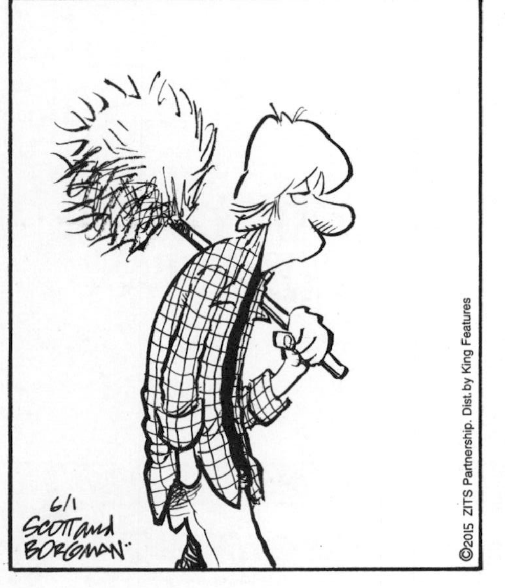
6/1
SCOTT and BORGMAN
©2015 ZITS Partnership. Dist. by King Features

DUST!
DUST!
DUST!

ROOM CLEAN?
CHECK.

PIERCE IS OUT. HECTOR IS OUT. SARA'S OUT. NATE IS OUT. SCOTT IS OUT. JASON'S OUT. ANGIE'S OUT. JAKE'S OUT.
SCOTT and BORGMAN 6/2

AARON'S OUT. TODD'S OUT. BRUCE'S OUT. JAMIE IS OUT.
©2015 ZITS Partnership. Dist. by King Features

(SIGH!) DO YOU WANT TO PLAY DISC GOLF, DAD?
AAAAND THE BOTTOM OF THE BARREL HAS BEEN SCRAPED.

Jerry: Hardware stores are time-warps for old guys.

SCOTT and BORGMAN 6/4

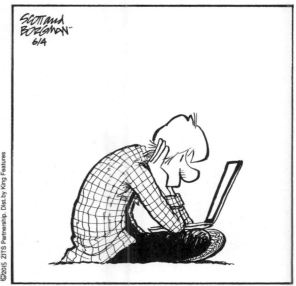

Jim: So sue me, I like Yahtzee.

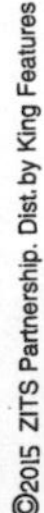
©2015 ZITS Partnership. Dist. by King Features

©2015 ZITS Partnership. Dist. by King Features

ZITS®
by JERRY SCOTT and JIM BORGMAN
G.P.A.
COLLEGE
GRAD SCHOOL
I WISH MOM WOULD LIGHTEN UP ON THE EXPECTATIONS.
I WOULDN'T COUNT ON THAT.
CAREER
6/7 SCOTT and BORGMAN
©2015 ZITS Partnership. Dist. by King Features

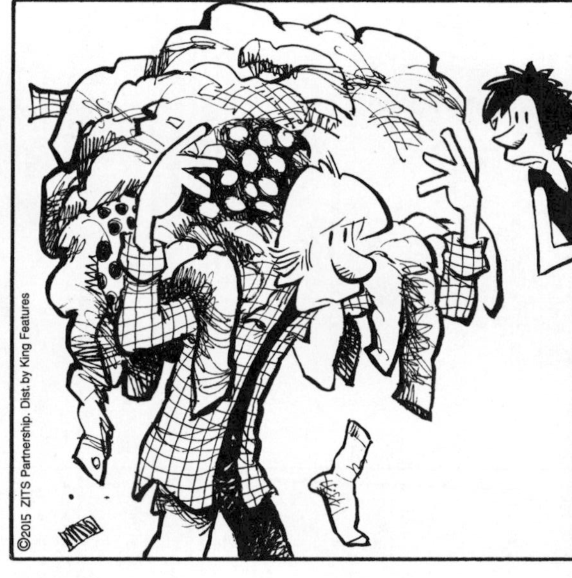

Jim: This has nothing to do with my daughter's car.

©2015 ZITS Partnership. Dist. by King Features

HEY! WHAT ARE YOU DOING??
TRANS-FERRING PRESSURE.
6/10
SCOTT and BORGMAN

©2015 ZITS Partnership. Dist. by King Features

PRACTICING?
ACTUALLY, I'M WRITING A SONG FOR MOM'S BIRTHDAY.
6/12
WOW. SHE'LL LOVE THAT!
YEAH. AND IT'S BEEN PRETTY EASY.
SCOTT and BORGMAN
©2015 ZITS Partnership. Dist. by King Features
YOU'D BE SURPRISED HOW MANY THINGS RHYME WITH "NAG."
SCOTT and BORGMAN 6/13
©2015 ZITS Partnership. Dist. by King Features
THIS IS WHY "HAPPY BIRTHDAY" ISN'T PLAYED WITH A LEAD GUITAR PART.

©2015 ZITS Partnership. Dist. by King Features

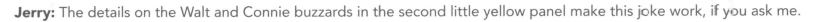

Jerry: The details on the Walt and Connie buzzards in the second little yellow panel make this joke work, if you ask me.

SCOTT and BORGMAN 6/15

SORRY, NANCY. I'LL TAKE CARE OF IT.

©2015 ZITS Partnership. Dist. by King Features

REALLY? NIGHT-MOWING?
IT'S SAFER FOR ME TO OPERATE MACHINERY WHEN I'M WIDE AWAKE.

IT'S HOT...
SCOTT and BORGMAN

...YOU'RE ALWAYS TELLING ME TO STAY HYDRATED...

©2015 ZITS Partnership. Dist. by King Features

...AND YOU WOULDN'T BELIEVE HOW MANY TRIPS TO THE KITCHEN I'M SAVING.
LOSE. THE. HOSE.
6/16

I'M GOING TO SEE IF MY PARENTS WILL BUY ME A NEW CAR.
WILL THEY DO IT?
ONLY IF I ASK THE RIGHT WAY.
6/17
SCOTT and BORGMAN
©2015 ZITS Partnership. Dist. by King Features
WHAT WAY IS THAT?
"WILL YOU BUY ME A MOTORCYCLE?"

WILL YOU BUY ME A MOTORCYCLE?
NO.
6/18

SO, YOU'LL BUY ME A CAR, INSTEAD?
NO.
©2015 ZITS Partnership. Dist. by King Features
YOU GUYS DON'T KNOW HOW TO PLAY THIS GAME!
AND YET, WE'RE WINNING.
SCOTT and BORGMAN

Jim: My partner Jerry was the head dweebmaster for Up With People in 1972, but he'll deny it if you ask him.
Jerry: I deny it.

by JERRY SCOTT and JIM BORGMAN

©2015 ZITS Partnership. Dist. by King Features

Jerry: I don't make up jokes for this strip as much as I just write down stuff that happens at home. And in the car.

ARE YOU WORKING THIS SUMMER, PIERCE?
NOT LIKELY.

I DON'T KNOW THE RIGHT PEOPLE.

WHO ARE THE RIGHT PEOPLE?
SWIMSUIT MODELS WHO'D PAY ME TO HOLD THEIR ROBES.
6/24
SCOTT and BORGMAN
©2015 ZITS Partnership. Dist by King Features

HAVE YOU CONSIDERED GETTING A JOB WAITING TABLES THIS SUMMER?
THEY SAY THE TRAINING IS GRUELING.
SCOTT and BORGMAN
6/25
©2015 ZITS Partnership. Dist. by King Features

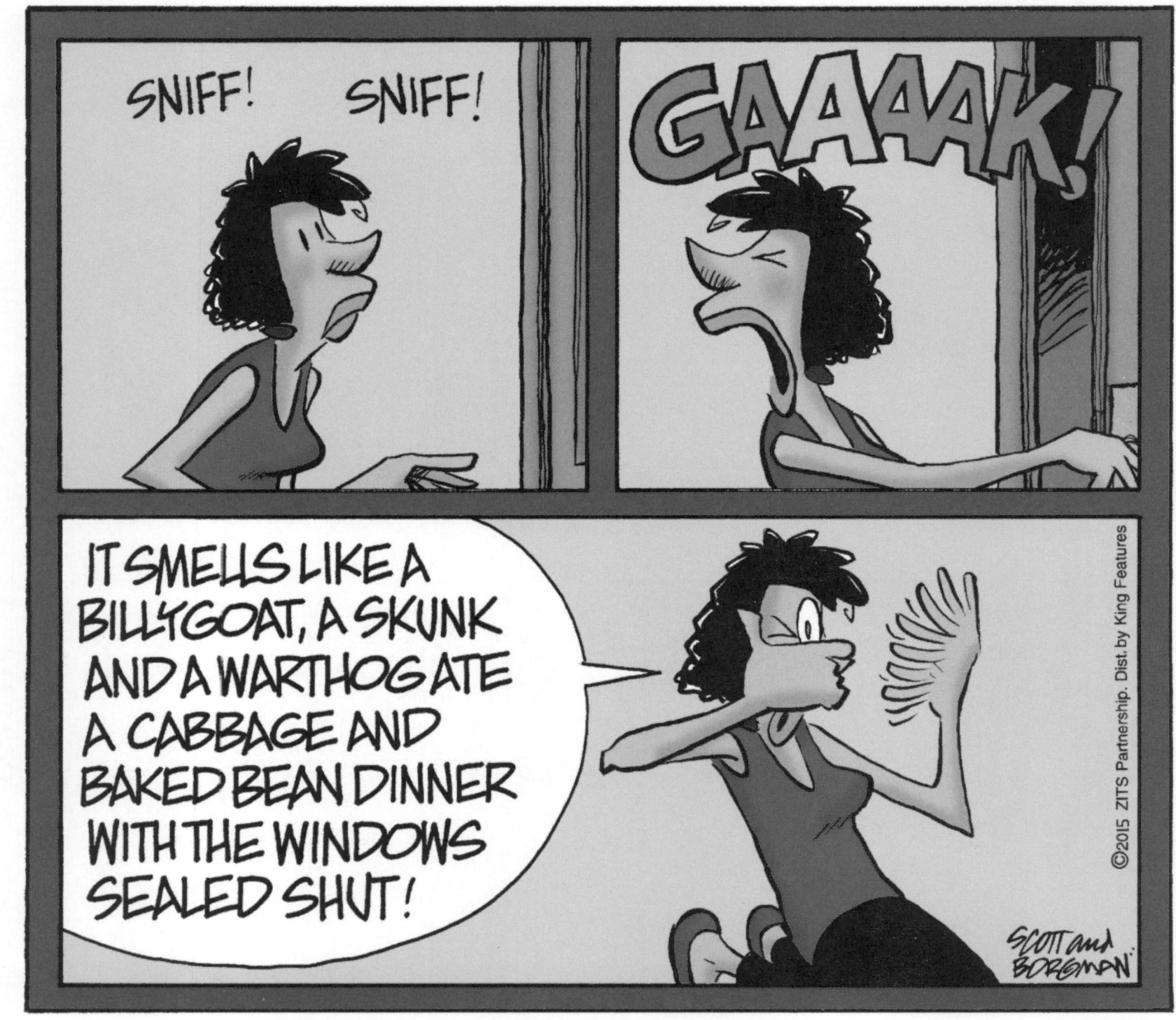

Jerry: I remember that smell.

REAL SUBTLE, MOM.
GASP!
ANY LESS ACCURATE AND THAT WOULD HAVE BEEN ALMOST INSULTING!
6/28

©2015 ZITS Partnership. Dist. by King Features

©2015 ZITS Partnership. Dist. by King Features

Jerry: Can I get an amen from you JVM210c Marshall amp owners out there?

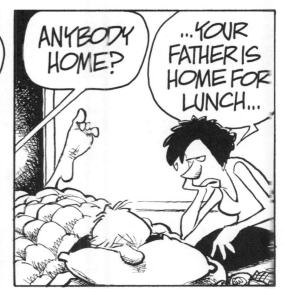

©2015 ZITS Partnership. Dist. by King Features

©2015 ZITS Partnership. Dist. by King Features

©2015 ZITS Partnership. Dist. by King Features

©2015 ZITS Partnership. Dist. by King Features

THIS IS HOW YOU WASH A CAR?
WOULD YOU MIND FLIPPING IT AROUND FOR ME?
SCOTT and BORGMAN
7/3
©2015 ZITS Partnership. Dist. by King Features

SCOTT and BORGMAN 7/4

©2015 ZITS Partnership. Dist. by King Features

HOT GIRLS SHOULD BE REQUIRED TO STAY IN ONE SPOT.
I'LL SIGN THAT PETITION.

ZITS®
by JERRY SCOTT and JIM BORGMAN
I'M NOT GIVING UP ON MY DREAM!
ATTABOY, JEREMY!
I WONDER WHAT THAT MEANS...
IS HE SHOOTING FOR A PERFECT S.A.T. SCORE?
AN IVY LEAGUE SCHOOL?
A CAREER IN MUSIC?
Z
IT MEANS THAT HE'S GOING BACK TO SLEEP.
7/5 SCOTT and BORGMAN
©2015 ZITS Partnership. Dist. by King Features

RUMOR!
I HEARD THAT A GIRL GOT ELECTROCUTED BY PUTTING A PHONE CHARGER IN HER MOUTH.
FACT:
THE GIRL GOT ELECTROCUTED BY PUTTING A PHONE CHARGER IN HER MOUTH WHILE MAKING TOAST IN THE BATHTUB.
SO IT WAS PARTLY TRUE!
7/6
SCOTT and BORGMAN
©2015 ZITS Partnership. Dist. by King Features

RUMOR!
EELSKIN WALLETS RUIN CREDIT CARDS BECAUSE OF THE LEFTOVER ELECTRICITY IN THE EELS.
FACT:
EELSKIN WALLETS ONLY RUIN CREDIT CARDS BY COSTING SO MUCH.
I WANT ONE.
SCOTT and BORGMAN 7/7
©2015 ZITS Partnership. Dist. by King Features

RUMOR!
I HEARD THAT THIS PLACE USES HORSEMEAT IN THEIR CHILI.
©2015 ZITS Partnership. Dist. by King Features

FACT:
THEY DON'T USE HORSEMEAT IN ANYTHING.
BUT THE FRENCH FRIES ARE COOKED IN THE BITTER TEARS OF HIGH SCHOOL GUIDANCE COUNSELORS.
MMM! SALTY!
7/8 SCOTT and BORGMAN

RUMOR!
PINEAPPLE JUICE STOPS A COUGH 500 TIMES BETTER THAN COUGH SYRUP!

FACT:
PINEAPPLE JUICE COMES FROM PINEAPPLES.
7/9 SCOTT and BORGMAN
©2015 ZITS Partnership. Dist. by King Features

JEREMY, YOU NEED TO MOW THE LAWN.
I'D LIKE TO, DAD.

BUT OUR GAS-POWERED MOWER WILL INCREASE MY CARBON FOOTPRINT, AND MY MORALS SIMPLY WON'T ALLOW IT.
SCOTT and BORGMAN 7/10

DIDN'T YOU JUST DRIVE YOUR VAN TO THE MAILBOX?
MY MORALS ARE TASK-SPECIFIC.
©2015 ZITS Partnership. Dist. by King Features

CANNONBALL!
SCOTT and BORGMAN 7/11

SPLOOSH!

HAVE YOU EVER THOUGHT OF JUST ORDERING A MEDIUM?
BIG
©2015 ZITS Partnership. Dist. by King Features

IF WE SOLD OUR HOUSE, WOULD I GET A CUT?
NO.

©2015 ZITS Partnership. Dist. by King Features

RIGHT??
I NEED TO MAKE A CALL.
FOR SALE
7/12 SCOTT and BORGMAN

©2015 ZITS Partnership. Dist. by King Features

©2015 ZITS Partnership. Dist. by King Features

WE HAVE TO GET JEREMY AND SARA OFF THE COUCH!
WHY DON'T YOU GO SUGGEST THEY PLAY A GAME?
GOOD IDEA!
BAD IDEA.
7/15
SCOTT and BORGMAN
©2015 ZITS Partnership. Dist. by King Features

JEREMY... SARA... DO YOU WANT TO HELP ME MAKE SOME POPCORN?
NO THANKS, WE'RE NOT REAL HUN
LY GRY.
THEY'VE GONE FROM FINISHING EACH OTHER'S SENTENCES TO FINISHING EACH OTHER'S SYLLABLES.
THAT'S IT. I'M GETTING THE HOSE.
7/16
SCOTT and BORGMAN
©2015 ZITS Partnership. Dist. by King Features

©2015 ZITS Partnership. Dist. by King Features

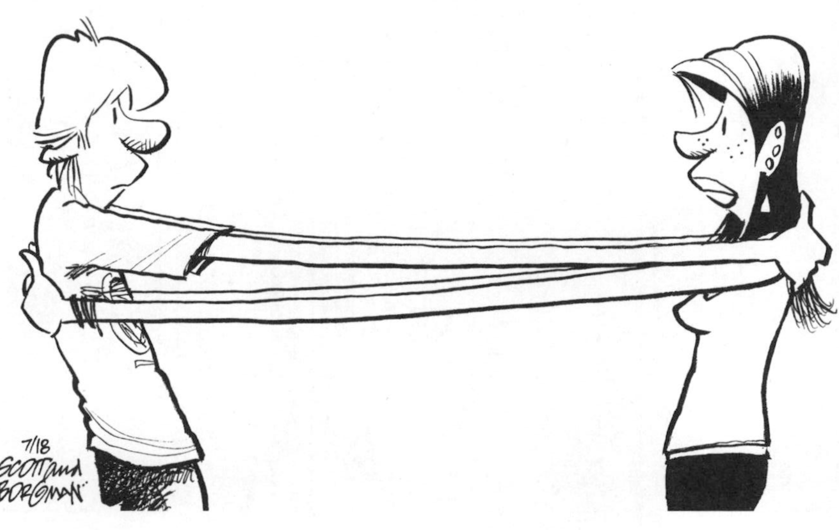

©2015 ZITS Partnership. Dist. by King Features

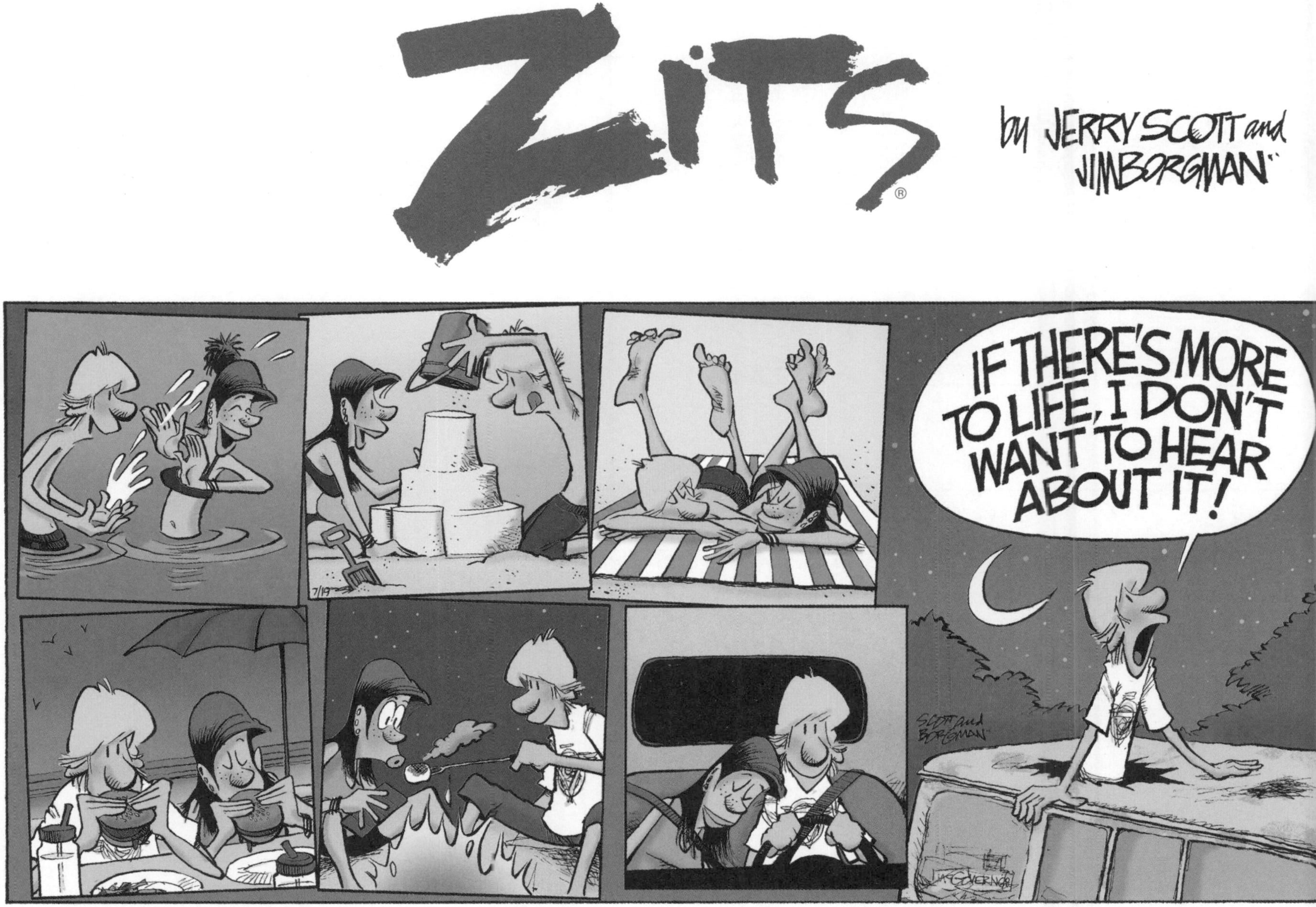

ZITS®
by JERRY SCOTT and JIM BORGMAN
IF THERE'S MORE TO LIFE, I DON'T WANT TO HEAR ABOUT IT!
SCOTT and BORGMAN

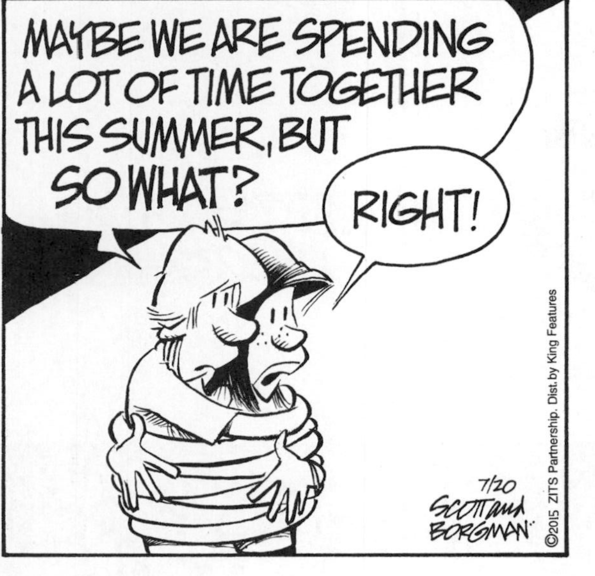
MAYBE WE ARE SPENDING A LOT OF TIME TOGETHER THIS SUMMER, BUT SO WHAT?
RIGHT!
©2015 ZITS Partnership. Dist. by King Features

HI JEREMYANDSARA!

AT LEAST WE'RE NOT AS BAD AS RICHANDAMY.
WAIT— ARE WE ONE WORD NOW, TOO?!

WE ARE NOT LIKE RICHANDAMY!
JEREMY, LOOK AT THE EVIDENCE!

WE'RE SPENDING SO MUCH TIME TOGETHER THAT PEOPLE HAVE STARTED THINKING OF US AS ONE ORGANISM!

I NEED TO FEEL MY OWN PROTOPLASM.
WAIT! COME BACK!
©2015 ZITS Partnership. Dist. by King Features

ON THE COUNT OF THREE, WE'RE GOING TO STOP BEING "JEREMYANDSARA" AND GO BACK TO BEING JEREMY AND SARA.
OKAY.
ONE... TWO...
7/22
SCOTT and BORGMAN
...THREE!
NOT BAD, RIGHT?
I CAN TASTE MY OWN SALIVA AGAIN!
©2015 ZITS Partnership. Dist. by King Features

WHOA! LET ME HELP YOU WITH THOSE GROCERIES, MRS. DUNCAN!
THANK YOU, HECTOR!
©2015 ZITS Partnership. Dist. by King Features

7/23
SCOTT and BORGMAN
YES. "THANK YOU," HECTOR.
NOBODY GIVES BETTER DIRTY LOOKS THAN YOUR MOM.

©2015 ZITS Partnership. Dist. by King Features

©2015 ZITS Partnership. Dist. by King Features

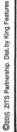

©2015 ZITS Partnership. Dist. by King Features

JEREMY, AREN'T YOU GOING TO DO ANYTHING TODAY?
MOM, THIS IS MY DOWN-TIME.
SCOTT and BORGMAN 7/27
©2015 ZITS Partnership. Dist. by King Features
I SHOULDN'T ASK, BUT DON'T YOU NEED TO HAVE UP-TIME BEFORE YOU CAN HAVE DOWN-TIME?
NOT AT MY LEVEL OF EXPERIENCE.

SCOTT and BORGMAN 7/28
CHIPS
DOUBLE SALT!
ALL SNACK FOODS ARE SINGLE-SERVING IF YOU TRY HARD ENOUGH.
©2015 ZITS Partnership. Dist. by King Features

©2015 ZITS Partnership. Dist. by King Features

©2015 ZITS Partnership. Dist. by King Features

Jim: Pipkin's is the name of a real produce market where a kid in my family once worked. We usually fictionalize names, but what could be better than Pipkin's?

Jim: Every twenty years or so we like to do a strip just for the Greek majors.

WELL, JEREMY, I'VE LOOKED OVER YOUR APPLICATION.
PIPKIN'S
©2015 ZITS Partnership. Dist. by King Features

I JUST HAVE ONE QUESTION ABOUT YOUR REFERENCES...
SCOTT AND BORGMAN 8/3

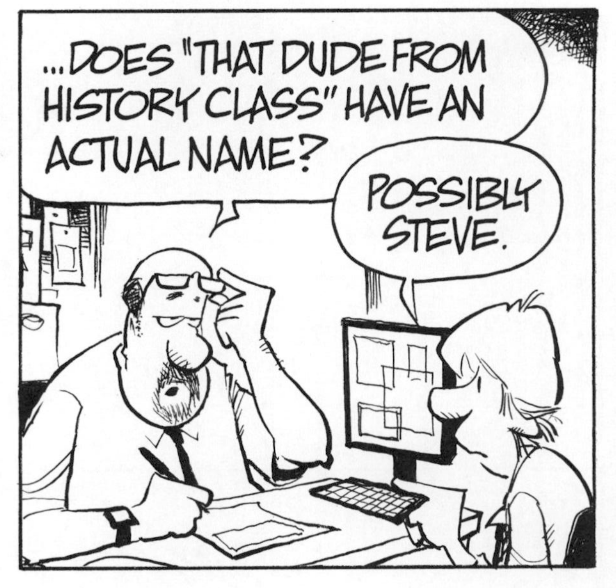
...DOES "THAT DUDE FROM HISTORY CLASS" HAVE AN ACTUAL NAME?
POSSIBLY STEVE.

SO, I GOT THE JOB AT PIPKIN'S.
OH, JEREMY! THAT'S GREAT!
©2015 ZITS Partnership. Dist. by King Features
THERE WERE FIVE OTHER APPLICANTS, BUT THEY PICKED ME.
WOW!
HOW DID YOU MAKE SUCH A GOOD IMPRESSION?
I WAS THE ONLY ONE WHO SHOWED UP FOR AN INTERVIEW.
8/4 SCOTT AND BORGMAN

YOUR LIPS ARE AMAZING!
MORE DETAILS, PLEASE.
SCOTT and BORGMAN
©2015 ZITS Partnership. Dist. by King Features
THEY'RE SO MOIST AND FULL AND ROSE PETAL PINK...
...THAT I ALMOST DON'T NOTICE THAT BLACKHEAD IN THE CORNER THAT NEVER GOES AWAY.
THAT'S ENOUGH DETAILS.
8/5

I GOT A COMFORTABLE SUBURBAN HOME, BABY.
DAA-DAA-DA-DUMM!
FOOD IN THE FRIDGE!
DAA-DAA-DA-DUMM!
MY PARENTS ARE LOVING AND REASONABLY SUPPORTIVE OF ME, HONEY.
DAA-DAA-DA------
©2015 ZITS Partnership. Dist. by King Features
SCOTT and BORGMAN 8/6
THIS IS NOT WORKING.
YOUR BLUES ARE LIKE, PERIWINKLE, DUDE.

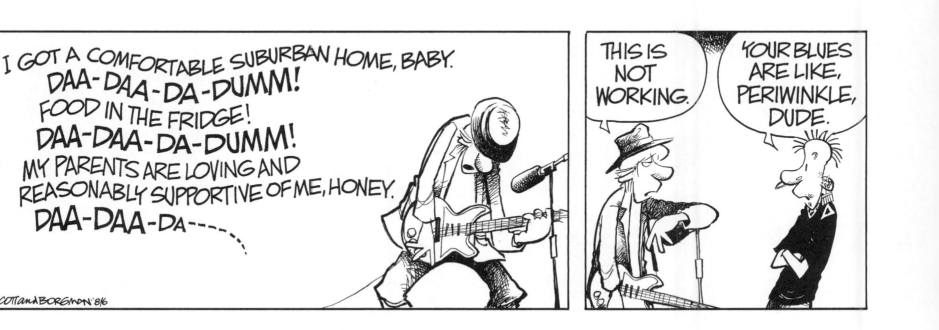

©2015 ZITS Partnership. Dist. by King Features

©2015 ZITS Partnership. Dist. by King Features

ZITS®
by JERRY SCOTT and JIM BORGMAN
HERE. I MADE YOU A CARD.
THANKS, JEREMY!
DAD
"HAPPY BIRTHDAY, DAD."
SCOTT and BORGMAN
WAIT--
I'M NOT DONE.
SNATCH!
8/9
"I LOVE YOU AND STUFF."
AWWW!
IT'S THE AFTERTHOUGHT THAT COUNTS.
©2015 ZITS Partnership. Dist. by King Features

©2015 ZITS Partnership. Dist. by King Features

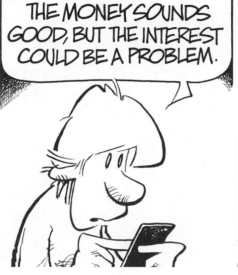

©2015 ZITS Partnership. Dist. by King Features

FINISHED PAINTING ALREADY?
I HAD TO STOP BECAUSE OF THE WEATHER.
SCOTT and BORGMAN 8/12
IT'S WARM AND SUNNY.
YEAH. I'M GOING TO THE LAKE.
©2015 ZITS Partnership. Dist. by King Features

HOW AM I SUPPOSED TO GET THE STUPID PAINT OUT OF THIS BRUSH?

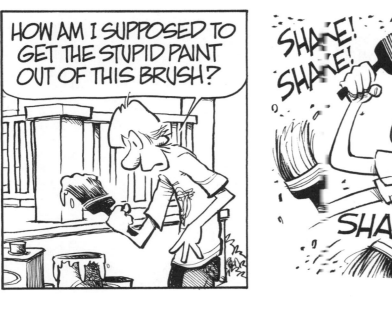

SHAKE!
SHAKE!
SHAKE!
SHAKE!
SCOTT and BORGMAN 8/13
THERE! THAT'S BETTER.
EVENING.
©2015 ZITS Partnership. Dist. by King Features

DAD, YOU STILL OWE ME FOR PAINTING THE PORCH.
Hard Rock CAFE BUCYRUS

I USED THAT MONEY TO GET THE PAINT OFF MY CAR.
Hard Rock
8/14

©2015 ZITS Partnership. Dist. by King Features
SO I DID ALL THAT WORK FOR NOTHING?
AND SOMEHOW YOU WERE STILL OVERPAID.
SCOTT and BORGMAN

Jim: Bucyrus, Ohio, does not really have a Hard Rock Cafe, but it does have a three-day bratwurst festival, so there's that.

I FEEL SORRY FOR SUPER-HOT GIRLS.

THEY MUST GET REALLY TIRED OF GUYS STARING AT THEM.
8/15
SCOTT and BORGMAN

©2015 ZITS Partnership. Dist. by King Features
LIKE YOU'RE DOING?
DUDE, I'M STARING WITH EMPATHY!

ZITS®
by JERRY SCOTT and JIM BORGMAN™

MOM, WE NEED TO TALK.

8/16
©2015 ZITS Partnership. Dist. by King Features
TISSUES
SCOTT and BORGMAN

OKAY, WHAT'S ON YOUR MIND?
THE WAY YOU OVERDO EVERYTHING.
TISSUES

WELL, I'M GOING TO WORK.
THUNK!
THAT WAS SO BEAUTIFUL! SAY THOSE WORDS AGAIN!
LATER, DAD.
8/17
SCOTT and BORGMAN
©2015 ZITS Partnership. Dist. by King Features

JEREMY! HOW WAS YOUR FIRST DAY OF WORK?
GOOD. I UNPACKED CRATES OF CANTALOUPE.
IF I DO WELL, THEY'LL MOVE ME UP TO MELON CHUCKER!
SCOTT and BORGMAN
8/18
CAN YOU BELIEVE I'LL GET PAID TO SMASH MELONS INTO A DUMPSTER?
YOU'RE LIVING THE DREAM.
©2015 ZITS Partnership. Dist. by King Features

YOU HAVE A NAMETAG ALREADY?
COOL, HUH?
I STARTED OUT WITH A PAPER ONE, AND THEY GAVE ME THIS WHEN MY SHIFT WAS OVER.
PLASTIC IS A SIGN OF RESPECT.
8/19
SCOTT and BORGMAN
©2015 ZITS Partnership. Dist. by King Features

HEY PIERCE, WHAT ARE YOU DOING HERE?
JUST HAVING A FEW GRAPES.
KIWI
APRICOT
MUSH MELON
AS A TRUSTED EMPLOYEE OF PIPKIN'S FRUIT MARKET, I HAVE TO ASK YOU TO LEAVE.

I LIKED YOU BETTER WHEN YOU WEREN'T "THE MAN."
THIS ISN'T JUST A NAME TAG, IT'S A BADGE!
8/20
SCOTT and BORGMAN
©2015 ZITS Partnership. Dist. by King Features

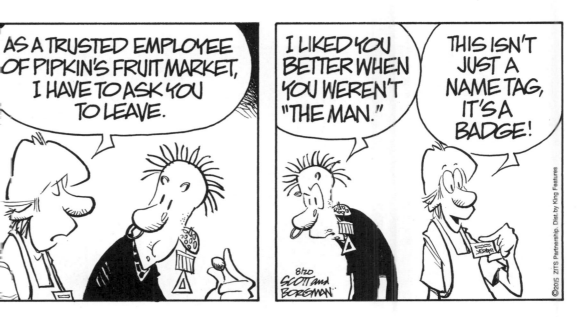

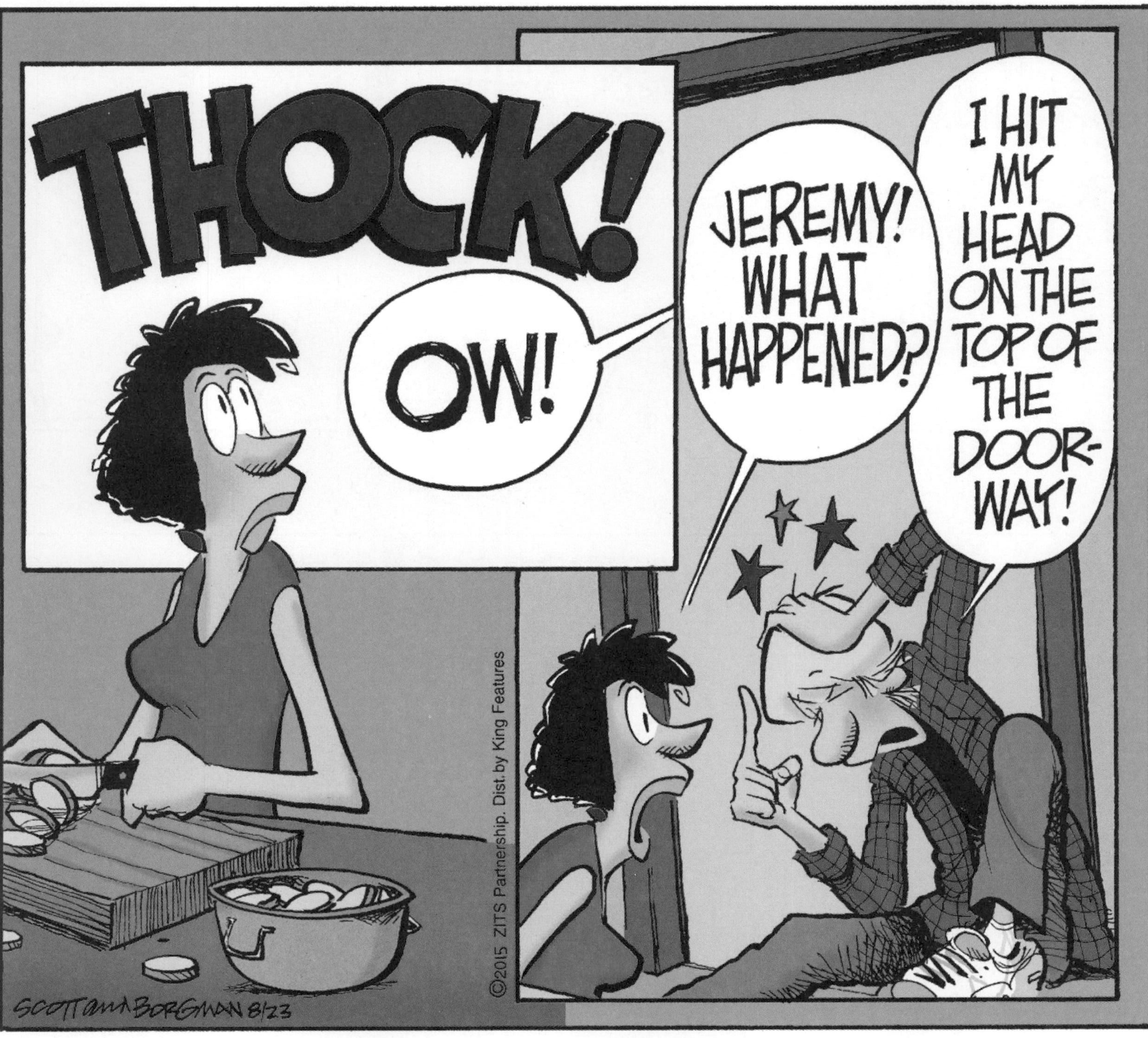
THOCK!
OW!
JEREMY! WHAT HAPPENED?
I HIT MY HEAD ON THE TOP OF THE DOOR-WAY!
SCOTT and BORGMAN 8/23
©2015 ZITS Partnership. Dist. by King Features

HOW??
I JUMPED AS HIGH AS I COULD TO SEE IF I COULD HIT MY HEAD ON THE TOP OF THE DOORWAY.
OKAY... NOW **I** HAVE A HEAD-ACHE.
MAYBE I SHOULD GO FOR THE CEILING NEXT.

JEREMY! YOU'RE LATE FOR WORK!
GAAAH!

THERE'S NOTHING WORSE THAN HAVING A JOB NIGHTMARE...
©2015 ZITS Partnership. Dist. by King Features

JEREMY! YOU'RE LATE FOR WORK!
...EXCEPT LIVING ONE.
SCOTT and BORGMAN

Jerry: The idea for this strip came from a reader, and I promised to acknowledge them by name. Thanks, reader!

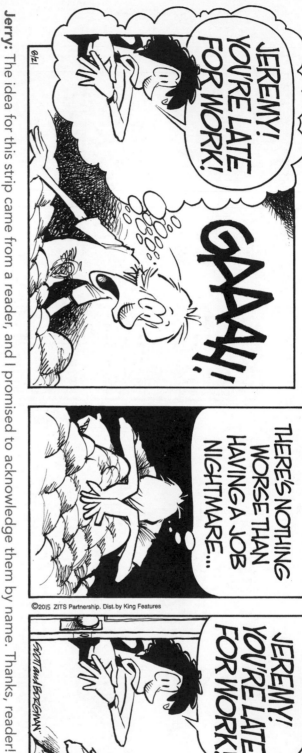

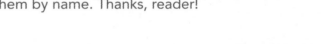

JEREMY, IT'S ALMOST TIME TO GO... ARE YOU PACKED?
NO.
WELL,
YEAH.
©2015 ZITS Partnership. Dist. by King Features

TECHNICALLY, I NEVER UNPACKED FROM LAST YEAR'S TRIP.
I'LL GO PRE-FREAK YOUR MOTHER OUT.
SCOTT and BORGMAN

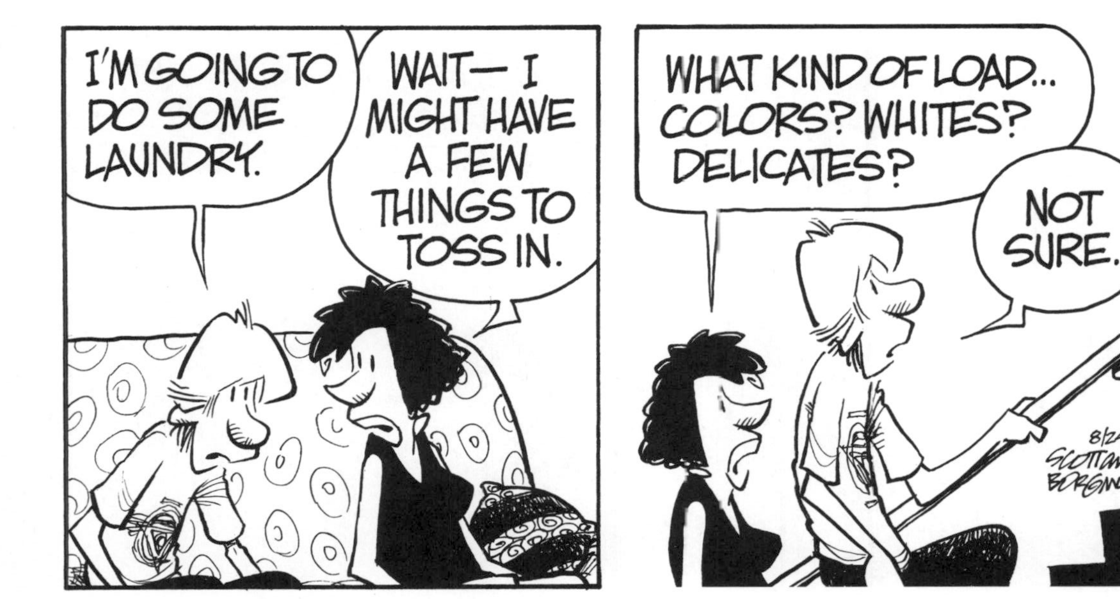

©2015 ZITS Partnership. Dist. by King Features

©2015 ZITS Partnership. Dist. by King Features

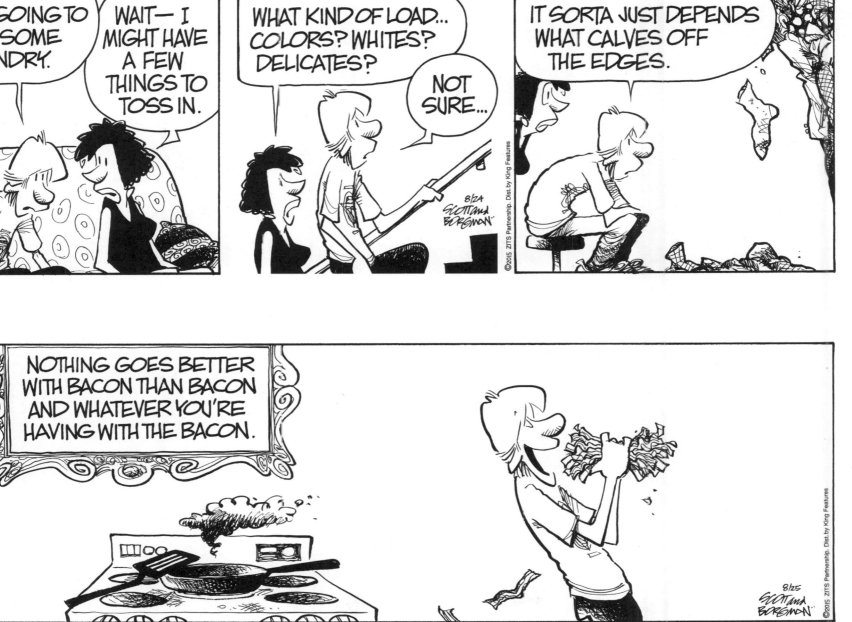

©2015 ZITS Partnership. Dist. by King Features
©2015 ZITS Partnership. Dist. by King Features

Jerry: I don't condone foul language in the comics, but come on! This works!

JEREMY, YOUR DAD AND I HAVE BEEN REVIEWING YOUR S.A.T. RESULTS.
WE DON'T EXPECT YOU TO GET A PERFECT SCORE.
AND WE DON'T EXPECT YOU TO GET INTO HARVARD.
SCOTT and BORGMAN 8/28
BUT YOU NEED TO TAKE THE TEST AGAIN.
WHY? I'VE MET ALL OF YOUR EXPECTATIONS. 
©2015 ZITS Partnership. Dist. by King Features
MY PARENTS ARE MAKING ME TAKE THE S.A.T. AGAIN, TOO.
WHY? WHAT DID YOU MESS UP?
©2015 ZITS Partnership. Dist. by King Features
I GOT LIKE, ZERO POINTS ON MY ESSAY.
HOW DID THAT HAPPEN?
8/29 SCOTT and BORGMAN
I DREW THREE PAGES OF FLAMING SKULLS.
THEY ALWAYS SLAM YOU FOR CREATIVITY.

by JERRY SCOTT and JIM BORGMAN

©2015 ZITS Partnership. Dist. by King Features

HAVE YOU EVER HAD A LIFE-CHANGING EXPERIENCE, MOM?
SURE! WHEN I GAVE BIRTH TO YOU.
SCOTT and BORGMAN 9/14
MINE WAS MY FIRST TRIPLE-MEAT PIZZA.
OH, SURE. SAME THING.
©2015 ZITS Partnership. Dist. by King Features

REMEMBER WHEN WE HAD JEREMY'S BABY SHOES HANGING FROM THE OLD SUBARU'S REAR-VIEW MIRROR?
©2015 ZITS Partnership. Dist. by King Features

NOW I BET I COULD PARK MY PRIUS IN ONE OF HIS SNEAKERS.
SCOTT and BORGMAN
9/15

I THINK I'LL GRIND MY SKATEBOARD DOWN THIS RAILING IN MY UNDER-WEAR WHILE WEARING THIS CHEESEHEAD.

I JUST HOPE NOBODY HAS DONE IT ALREADY TODAY.
INSTAGRAM IS GETTING WAY TOO COMPETETIVE.
SCOTT and BORGMAN 9/16
©2015 ZITS Partnership. Dist. by King Features

HOW'S THE BRAKE JOB COMING, BOYS?
WE'RE WATCHING A YOUTUBE VIDEO.

YOU SHOULD PROBABLY WATCH SEVERAL.
OKAY.

©2015 ZITS Partnership. Dist. by King Features

CAR REPAIR CAN BE TRICKY!
BUT THIS IS A BIKINI FAIL VIDEO.
WE'LL TAKE HIS ADVICE ANYWAY.
9/17
SCOTT and BORGMAN

Jerry: I have learned how to do so many things by watching YouTube videos . . . some of them useful.

JEREMY, WE--
Z
SHHH! MOM, I'M SLEEPWALKING.
YOU ARE NOT!
I AM. SO YOU CAN'T NAG ME ABOUT ANYTHING.
COME BACK HERE!
Z
AFTER I SLEEP-EAT BREAKFAST.
©2015 ZITS Partnership. Dist. by King Features
9/18
SCOTT and BORGMAN

JEREMY DOESN'T WANT TO TALK TO ME, SO HE CLAIMS TO BE SLEEP-EATING.
Z
REALLY?

CHEWING WITH HIS MOUTH CLOSED... NO SNARKY ATTITUDE...
©2015 ZITS Partnership. Dist. by King Features

LET'S HOPE THERE'S NO CURE.
SCOTT and BORGMAN
9/19

ZITS®
by JERRY SCOTT and JIM BORGMAN

SEE YOU TWO IN A WHILE!
STUDY HARD!
WE WILL.

I'M GLAD THAT YOUR PARENTS TRUST US IN YOUR ROOM.
YEAH, TRUST.

WHO WANTS SNICKER-DOODLES AND MILK?

©2015 ZITS Partnership. Dist. by King Features

DID I LEAVE MY HAMMER IN HERE?

TRUST MIXED WITH CONSTANT SURVEILLANCE.
SCOTT and BORGMAN 9/20

Jerry: I think I meant to say "equinox," not "solst ce" here.

Jerry: Oh, wait. I did a joke about this 103 pages ago.

ALL I DID WAS TOSS JEREMY'S GYM CLOTHES IN WITH THE LOAD!
WHO KNEW A WASHER COULD GAG?
SCOTT and BORGMAN 9/25
©2015 ZITS Partnership. Dist. by King Features

WOULD YOU RATHER I SAT AROUND DOING NOTHING?
SCOTT and BORGMAN 9/26
©2015 ZITS Partnership. Dist. by King Features

©2015 ZITS Partnership. Dist. by King Features

TIME FOR MY WEEKLY SHOWER!
DOES THAT MEAN YOU SHOWER ONCE A WEEK, OR THAT THIS SHOWER WILL BE A WEEK LONG?
MAYBE THIS WATER BILL CAN PROVIDE SOME CLUES...
9/28
SCOTT and BORGMAN
©2015 ZITS Partnership. Dist. by King Features

I THOUGHT YOU SAID YOU WERE LATE BECAUSE THE VAN WOULDN'T START!
UH, YEAH, THAT WAS PART OF IT.
JEREMY, DON'T LIE TO ME!
I DIDN'T LIE!
I JUST BOTOXED THE TRUTH.
©2015 ZITS Partnership. Dist. by King Features
9/29
SCOTT and BORGMAN

MY MOM SAVES EVERYTHING.
SCOTT and BORGMAN

I THINK WE STILL HAVE EVERY DRAWING I EVER MADE.
I DOUBT IT.

DON'T.
OKAY, I UN-DOUBT IT.
©2015 ZITS Partnership. Dist. by King Features
9/30

SUGARCANE?
YEAH. THE LITTLE SPOON IN THE BOWL WAS TAKING TOO LONG.
WALK THE MOON
10/1
SCOTT and BORGMAN
©2015 ZITS Partnership. Dist. by King Features

THE MIGRATORY SEASON IS UPON US.
UPON YOU, SPECIFICALLY.
SCOTT and BORGMAN 10/2
©2015 ZITS Partnership. Dist. by King Features

Jerry: I think this is what happens when you try to write a comic strip while taking cold medicine.

JEREMY, PUT YOUR PHONE DOWN WHILE I'M TALKING TO YOU.
I CAN HEAR YOU.
©2015 ZITS Partnership. Dist. by King Features
NO, REALLY. THIS IS IMPORTANT.
I'M LISTENING.
EYE CONTACT IS A PART OF CONVERSATION!
NOW I'M LISTENING AND CREEPED OUT.
SCOTT and BORGMAN 10/3

©2015 ZITS Partnership. Dist. by King Features

SCOTT and BORGMAN 10/4
THANK YOU, JEREMY. I REALLY APPRECIATE THE
HELP.
ANYTHING ELSE?

ONE OF THE COOL THINGS ABOUT WORKING HERE IS THAT WE'RE ALLOWED TO EAT ANY FOOD THAT DOESN'T COME WRAPPED IN PLASTIC.
WAIT-- THERE'S FOOD THAT DOESN'T COME WRAPPED IN PLASTIC??
SCOTT and BORGMAN 10/5
©2015 ZITS Partnership. Dist. by King Features

SCOTT and BORGMAN 10/6
©2015 ZITS Partnership. Dist. by King Features
WORK IS GOOD.
Z

I'M HOME!
ARE YOU HUNGRY, JEREMY?
NAW. I ATE A BUNCH OF SNAP PEAS AND MANGOES AT WORK, SO I'M STUFFED.
©2015 ZITS Partnership. Dist. by King Features

10/7
SCOTT AND BORGMAN

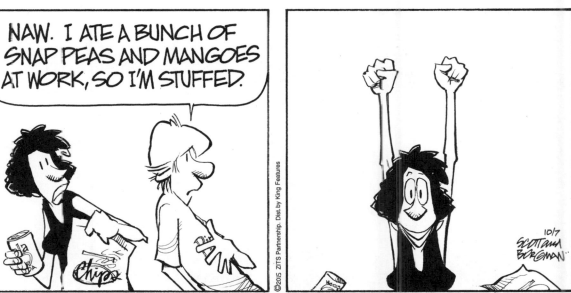

THIS JOB IS REALLY GOOD FOR ME.
10/8
SCOTT AND BORGMAN
©2015 ZITS Partnership. Dist. by King Features

I CAN'T BELIEVE HOW MUCH I LIKE WORKING...
...FOR OTHER PEOPLE.
NO NEED TO CLARIFY.

OKAY! OKAY! I SCREWED UP AGAIN, BUT I HAVE A GOOD REASON.
WHICH IS...?
I'M SEVENTEEN.
THE INSANITY DEFENSE?
WELL, THERE'S PLENTY OF EVIDENCE TO SUPPORT IT!

©2015 ZITS Partnership. Dist. by King Features

Jerry: Actually, it's the undeveloped prefrontal cortex defense.

©2015 ZITS Partnership. Dist. by King Features

by JERRY SCOTT and JIM BORGMAN

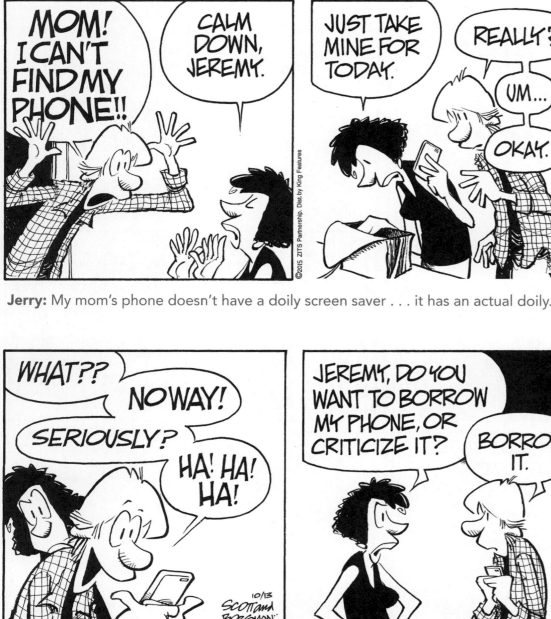

Jerry: My mom's phone doesn't have a doily screen saver . . . it has an actual doily.

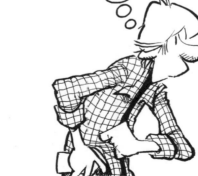

JEREMY! I'VE BEEN TEXTING YOU ALL MORNING!
SORRY. I LOST MY PHONE.
10/14
SCOTT and BORGMAN
BUT MY MOM LET ME BORROW HERS.
PLING! TIME TO TAKE YOUR HORMONE PILLS!
MY INSINCERE CONDOLENCES.
HOW MUCH TO BUY YOUR SILENCE?
©2015 ZITS Partnership. Dist. by King Features

I CAN'T BELIEVE THAT I HAD TO BORROW MY MOM'S PHONE TODAY.
10/15
SCOTT and BORGMAN
OH, WELL... I GUESS HER PHONE IS BETTER THAN NO PHONE.

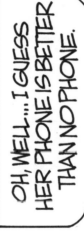

ODD... WHY IS JEREMY'S MOM SENDING ME HORNY DEVIL EMOJIS?
©2015 ZITS Partnership. Dist. by King Features

YOU JUST GOT A TEXT FROM YOUR DAD.
I BET HE DOESN'T KNOW THAT I HAVE MY MOM'S PHONE.
BZZZZ

I CAN'T LOOK! IT MIGHT BE DISTURBING!
IT JUST SAYS THAT HE'S COMING HOME FOR LUNCH...
10/16
SCOTT and BORGMAN

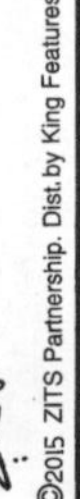
©2015 ZITS Partnership. Dist. by King Features

...AND THAT YOU'RE A STONE-COLD FOX.
I THINK I'M GONNA BE SICK!

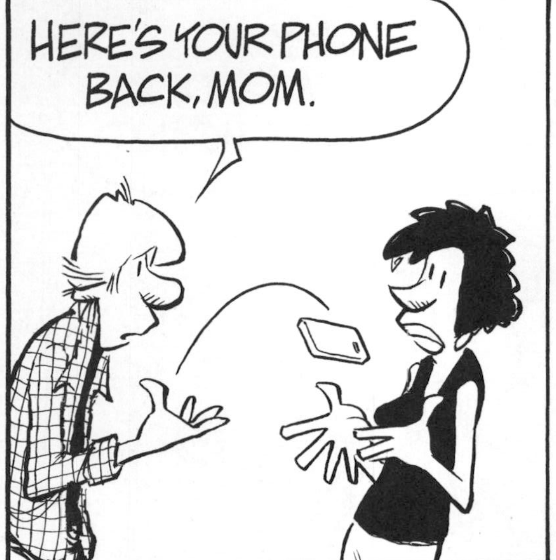

HERE'S YOUR PHONE BACK, MOM.
ALL I DID WAS CHANGE THE SCREEN SAVER, DELETE SOME PHOTOS, ADD A FEW APPS, UPDATE YOUR OPERATING SYSTEM, AND CHANGE ALL OF YOUR PASSWORDS.
10/17
SCOTT and BORGMAN

©2015 ZITS Partnership. Dist. by King Features

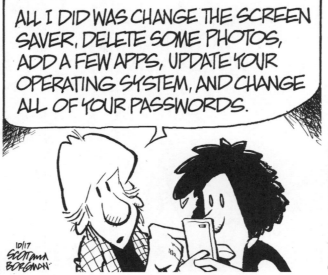

THIS BEARS NO RESEMBLANCE TO MY OLD PHONE!
YOU'RE WELCOME.

Jim: Just being helpful. Otherwise known as total lack of boundaries.

©2015 ZITS Partnership. Dist. by King Features

Jim: This is called character exposition. Hector is revealed as a neat freak. At least until this series ends.

©2015 ZITS Partnership. Dist. by King Features

©2015 ZITS Partnership. Dist. by King Features

©2015 ZITS Partnership. Dist. by King Features

©2015 ZITS Partnership. Dist. by King Features

Jerry: Moms! A helpful time-saving tip!

Jim: Ah, Nightmare #17.

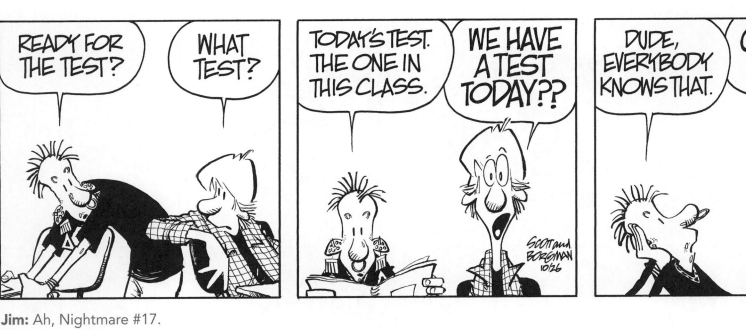

Jerry: You can look up the definition of "flench" in the Urban Dictionary, but I wouldn't if I were you.

©2015 ZITS Partnership. Dist. by King Features

ZITS®

by JERRY SCOTT and JIM BORGMAN

NOW WHERE DID I PUT MY PHONE?
WHY DID I JUST COME IN HERE?
DID--? SHOOT! I FORGOT WHAT I WAS GOING TO SAY.

JEREMY, HAVE YOU SEEN MY GLASSES ANYWHERE?
SCOTT and BORGMAN

©2015 ZITS Partnership. Dist. by King Features
THANK YOU...
AND BY THE WAY...

...YOU STILL HAVEN'T GIVEN ME THE CHANGE FROM THE TWENTY DOLLARS YOU TOOK OUT OF MY PURSE TWO WEEKS AGO TO BUY MILK ON YOUR WAY HOME FROM SARA'S HOUSE.
THAT SHE REMEMBERS...

WILL YOU ASK HIM?
THIS WAS YOUR IDEA... YOU ASK HIM!
©2015 ZITS Partnership. Dist. by King Features

FINE.
SCOTT AND BORGMAN

JEREMY, WILL YOU ACTIVATE OUR NEW "TEEN TRACKER" APP FOR ME, PLEASE?
IS THIS SOME KIND OF IRONY TEST?
11/2

JEREMY, THIS ISN'T ABOUT YOU OKAY?
11/3

BUT SOMETIMES I THINK YOU ACT LIKE A TOTAL NIMROD.
SCOTT AND BORGMAN

UM...
HEY, THIS IS MY PROBLEM! DON'T MAKE IT ABOUT YOU!
©2015 ZITS Partnership. Dist. by King Features

Jerry: Okay, not likely, but I love to see Jim draw abject horror on Jeremy's face once in a while.

CRUNCH! CRUNCH! CRUNCH!

©2015 ZITS Partnership. Dist. by King Features

MY HEARING LOSS ISN'T AGE-RELATED, IT'S TEENAGE-RELATED.

DO YOU RECOGNIZE THIS SHIRT?
IT'S YOURS. YOU WORE IT IN FIFTH GRADE.

THAT JUST GOES TO SHOW YOU THAT IF YOU TAKE CARE OF THINGS, THEY LAST.

©2015 ZITS Partnership. Dist. by King Features

WHERE DID YOU FIND IT?
IT OOZED OUT THE TOP OF MY LAUNDRY PILE.

Jerry: My nephew Ben was the inspiration for this strip. He's, like, thirty, and I'm pretty sure he's still grounded.

11/9
SCOTT and BORGMAN

GOT'M!
SLAM!

©2015 ZITS Partnership. Dist. by King Features

KEVIN...?

OH, KEVIN!
YOU NAMED A FLY "KEVIN"?

NAMED HIM?? I RAISED HIM IN MY LOCKER FROM THE TIME HE WAS A LARVA!
SCOTT and BORGMAN

©2015 ZITS Partnership. Dist. by King Features

IT'S ALWAYS BEEN MORE OF AN INCUBATOR THAN A LOCKER.
THAT EXPLAINS THE SMELL.
11/10

I'M SORRY I KILLED YOUR FLY, PIERCE.
HIS NAME WAS KEVIN.
HE LIKED YOU.
FLUSH!
OF ALL MY FRIENDS, HE SPREAD LESS FILTH AND DISEASE TO YOU THAN ANYBODY ELSE.
NOW I'M SORRY AND QUEASY.
©2015 ZITS Partnership. Dist. by King Features
SCOTT and BORGMAN
11/11

BAM! BAM! BAM!
CONGRATS ON YOUR NEW ZINE.
THANKS. REACTION HAS BEEN MIXED.
©2015 ZITS Partnership. Dist. by King Features
11/12
SCOTT and BORGMAN

©2015 ZITS Partnership. Dist. by King Features

©2015 ZITS Partnership. Dist. by King Features

ZITS®

by JERRY SCOTT and JIM BORGMAN

©2015 ZITS Partnership. Dist.by King Features

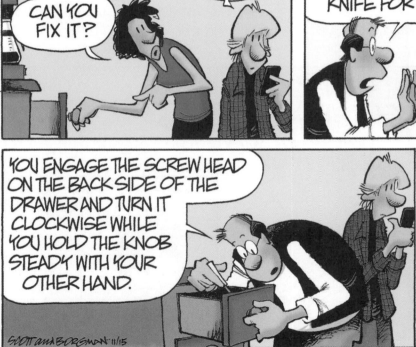

©2015 ZITS Partnership. Dist. by King Features

©2015 ZITS Partnership. Dist. by King Features

IS IT JUST ME, OR IS THIS DAY DRAGGING?
11/18

IT'S NOT YOU.
©2015 ZITS Partnership. Dist. by King Features
SCOTT AND BORGMAN

HI JEREMY!
THAT'S MY GIRLFRIEND!
11/19 SCOTT AND BORGMAN

HEY, GRIFF... IS IT COOL IF I MAKE SARA THINK I'M IN CHARGE OF SOMETHING?
GO FOR IT.

YOU'RE FIRING A BANANA?
I RUN A TIGHT SHIP.
©2015 ZITS Partnership. Dist. by King Features

©2015 ZITS Partnership. Dist. by King Features

LIKE WHAT?

DID YOU KNOW CRUNCHBERRIES AREN'T A REAL FOOD?

©2015 ZITS Partnership. Dist. by King Features

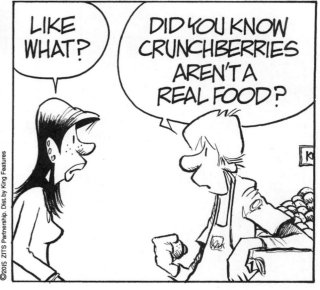

©2015 ZITS Partnership. Dist. by King Features

©2015 ZITS Partnership. Dist. by King Features

©2015 ZITS Partnership. Dist. by King Features

Jim: A sincere, kindhearted comic strip? Even we cartoonists are out of our comfort zones here.

©2015 ZITS Partnership. Dist. by King Features

YOU STAYED FOR THE WHOLE SONG!
HOW COME?
I NEED MY HAMMER.
SCOTT and BORGMAN 11/29

©2015 ZITS Partnership. Dist. by King Features

©2015 ZITS Partnership. Dist. by King Features

Jim: I love wondering what might have happened to prompt the response "Fry it, anyway."

BZZZZZ...
SMILE, EVERYBODY!
I'LL PAY YOU TEN BUCKS.
ALL THAT BUYS IS A SNEER.
SCOTT and BORGMAN 12/2
©2015 ZITS Partnership. Dist. by King Features

WELL, WE TOOK FORTY-SEVEN HOLIDAY CARD PHOTOS...
SCOTT and BORGMAN 12/3
©2015 ZITS Partnership. Dist. by King Features
...AND JEREMY SCOWLED IN FORTY-SIX OF THEM.
AND THEN THERE'S THIS ONE...
OOH... THAT IS NOT A HOLIDAY GESTURE!

©2015 ZITS Partnership. Dist. by King Features

Jerry: Where there's a will (and Wi-Fi), there's a way.

©2015 ZITS Partnership. Dist. by King Features

©2015 ZITS Partnership. Dist. by King Features

Jim: I often make expressions in the mirror in order to draw them right. For this one I had to take selfies.

THEN
LOOK AT THAT SMILE! WHO'S A HAPPY BOY? WHO'S A HAPPY BOY?
12/11
SCOTT and BORGMAN
©2015 ZITS Partnership. Dist. by King Features
NOW
LOOK AT THAT SMILE! WHAT ARE YOU UP TO?

HECTOR AND I GOT THE VAN'S HEATER WORKING.
SORT OF.
IT'S BLAZING HOT ON THE FLOOR AND FREEZING COLD EVERYWHERE ELSE,
BUT WE'LL FIGURE IT OUT.

AND SOON, I HOPE.
©2015 ZITS Partnership. Dist. by King Features
12/12
SCOTT and BORGMAN

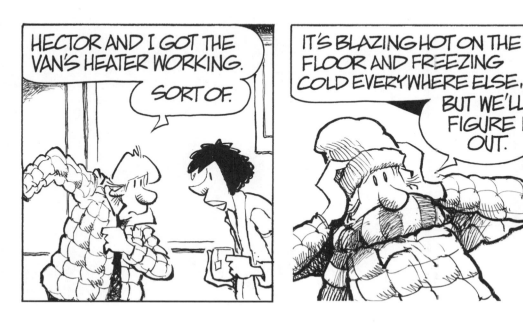

ZITS®
by JERRY SCOTT and JIM BORGMAN
HOW WAS YOUR DAY, JEREMY?
HOW WAS YOUR DAY, JEREMY?
HOW WAS YOUR DAY, JEREMY?
HOW WAS YOUR DAY, JEREMY?
HOW WAS YOUR DAY, JEREMY?
HOW W--
SCOTT and BORGMAN
©2015 ZITS Partnership. Dist. by King Features
12/13

I'VE BEEN TOTALLY FANTASIZING ABOUT STAR WARS!

©2015 ZITS Partnership. Dist. by King Features
LIKE, I'M HAN SOLO AND THE VAN IS MY MILLENNIUM FALCON!

THAT WOULD MAKE ME... CHEWBACCA?
BUT WAY LESS HAIRY AND WITH CUTE SHOES!
12/14
SCOTT and BORGMAN

SLAM!
12/15
SCOTT and BORGMAN

WHAM!
©2015 ZITS Partnership. Dist. by King Features
SOMEONE'S NOT IN A HOLIDAY MOOD.
"SOMEONE" HAS FOUR TESTS AND TWO PAPERS DUE BEFORE BREAK.
STOMP! STOMP! STOMP!

©2015 ZITS Partnership. Dist. by King Features

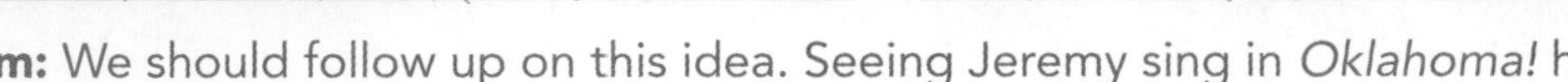
Jim: We should follow up on this idea. Seeing Jeremy sing in *Oklahoma!* has possibilities.

©2015 ZITS Partnership. Dist. by King Features

DO YOU THINK JEREMY FEELS OKAY?
WHY?
WELL, I WAS JUST TALKING TO HIM, AND UM...
WHAT?

HE DIDN'T ROLL HIS EYES ONCE.
I'M CALLING THE OPHTHALMOL-OGIST!
SCOTT AND BORGMAN 12/18
©2015 ZITS Partnership. Dist. by King Features

(GASP!) A SCARF!
DO YOU LIKE IT?
SCOTT AND BORGMAN 12/19
©2015 ZITS Partnership. Dist. by King Features

IT'S BEAUTIFUL! I LOVE IT, JEREMY!
YES!!

AND I'M SURE THE PIZZA SMELL WILL FADE.
I HAD TROUBLE FINDING A BOX.
Jake's Pizza

©2015 ZITS Partnership. Dist. by King Features

SO, THE VAN NEEDS A NEW CARBURETOR THAT COSTS ABOUT $250.
IS THAT WHAT YOU WANT FOR CHRISTMAS?

GIFT
CARDS
~~NO~~ YES.
12/21 SCOTT and BORGMAN

©2015 ZITS Partnership. Dist. by King Features

ALL I'M GETTING FOR CHRISTMAS IS A CARBURETOR FOR THE VAN?
THAT'S WHAT YOU ASKED FOR.
YEAH, I KNOW, BUT...
IT WAS A MATURE DECISION, JEREMY. YOU'RE GROWING UP!

WAS THAT A COMPLIMENT OR A WARNING?
12/22 SCOTT and BORGMAN

©2015 ZITS Partnership. Dist. by King Features

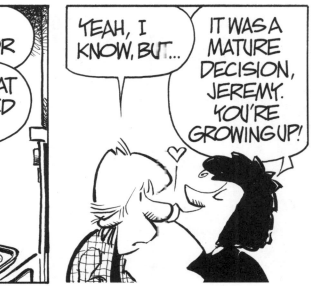

Jim: Why haven't we seen Sarta in a beanie before?

©2015 ZITS Partnership. Dist. by King Features

©2015 ZITS Partnership. Dist. by King Features

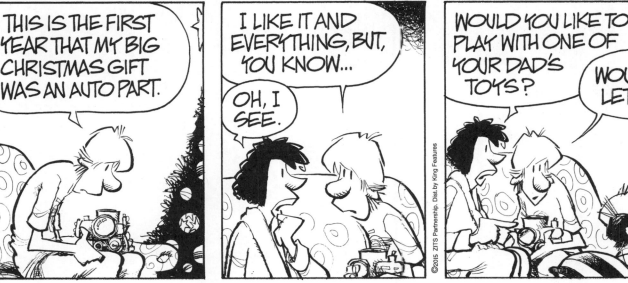

Jim: I think this is Jerry making fun of me again.

Jim: *Somebody* has to do it.

Jerry: Sorry, antiquarians. Just kidding.

Jerry: Ouch. It hurts when it's true.

GROWING A NEW YEARS BEARD, DAD?
MAYBE.
IT'S TRENDY.
AND MANLY.
SCOTT and BORGMAN 1/1
AND VERY CLOSE TO SLEEP-ON-THE-COUCHY.
THE VERDICT IS IN.
©2015 ZITS Partnership. Dist. by King Features
SO, YOU'RE GOING TO SHAVE THE BEARD?
YEAH. YOUR MOM HATES IT.
I THINK IT'S COOL. IT GIVES YOU A WHOLE NEW IDENTITY.
REALLY?
©2015 ZITS Partnership. Dist. by King Features
WALT DUNCAN: LUMBERJACK ORTHODONTIST!
SHHHKXT!
SCOTT and BORGMAN 1/2